'"Imagine, Create, Belong" is an exceptionally innovative 8-session program that fills a gap for neuro-diverse youth aged 11–15 who struggle with responding to and understanding social situations. It is both culturally and developmentally sensitive and identifies the importance of missing links in early foundational play development. A first of its kind, the program focusses on neuro-responsive social scaffolding using play-based movie-making activities. Engaging and fun, it is inclusive of neuro-diverse students in both mainstream and special-education settings. "Imagine, Create, Belong" presents breakthrough concepts in how to assist youth who struggle with social engagement. This is an essential program for all child and youth therapists!'

Lorri Yasenik, PhD, RSW, RPT-S, CPT-S,
Co-Director of Rocky Mountain Play Therapy Institute

Storying Beyond Social Difficulties with Neuro-Diverse Adolescents

Traditional approaches to social skill development may often be ineffective for those in most need of them – those who are neuro-diverse (for example, on the Autism Spectrum, with dyspraxia, or with Attention Deficit Hyperactivity Disorder), those who have experienced trauma, those with an intellectual disability, and those who present with Complex Communication Needs. This may be due to difficulties with language, attention, and memory.

Storying Beyond Social Difficulties with Neuro-Diverse Adolescents is a manual that outlines an eight-session programme, called "Imagine, Create, Belong", that involves a range of activities designed to develop theory of mind, flexible thinking, empathy, and narrative ability. The sessions can be run across 8 or 16 weeks and contain sections suitable for those in mainstream schools, with adaptations to support adolescents with additional needs (including moderate intellectual disability and Complex Communication Needs). The manual does this via a range of age-appropriate play-based activities within a group setting focused on making a movie. It includes non-verbal and verbal approaches to social development and is an implicit approach to social skills.

The programme is suitable for young people aged 11 years to 15 years with social difficulties. It includes content that may suit adolescents from both individualist and collectivist cultures. The manual provides step-by-step guidance for practitioners to run the "Imagine, Create, Belong" social skills programme with participants with a range of intellectual abilities who have been identified by parents, teachers, or other professionals as having social difficulties.

Sophie Goldingay is a senior lecturer and Associate Head of School, Teaching and Learning, in the School of Health and Social Development, Deakin University, Geelong, Australia.

Karen Stagnitti is Emeritus Professor in the School of Health and Social Development, Deakin University, Geelong, Australia.

Belinda Dean is a lecturer in Nursing at Deakin University, Geelong, Australia, and holds a Master's degree in Child Play Therapy.

Narelle Robertson is a researcher at the Centre for Project Evaluation at Melbourne University, Australia.

Donna Davidson is an occupational therapist and play therapist.

Eleanor Francis is a speech pathologist who has worked with children and adults in a variety of settings.

Storying Beyond Social Difficulties with Neuro-Diverse Adolescents

The "Imagine, Create, Belong" Social Development Programme

Sophie Goldingay, Karen Stagnitti,
Belinda Dean, Narelle Robertson,
Donna Davidson, and
Eleanor Francis

LONDON AND NEW YORK

First published 2020
by Routledge
2 Park Square, Milton Park, Abingdon, Oxon OX14 4RN

and by Routledge
52 Vanderbilt Avenue, New York, NY 10017

Routledge is an imprint of the Taylor & Francis Group, an informa business

© 2020 Sophie Goldingay, Karen Stagnitti, Belinda Dean, Narelle Robertson, Donna Davidson, & Eleanor Frances

The right of Sophie Goldingay, Karen Stagnitti, Belinda Dean, Narelle Robertson, Donna Davidson, & Eleanor Frances to be identified as authors of this work has been asserted by them in accordance with sections 77 and 78 of the Copyright, Designs and Patents Act 1988.

All rights reserved. No part of this book may be reprinted or reproduced or utilised in any form or by any electronic, mechanical, or other means, now known or hereafter invented, including photocopying and recording, or in any information storage or retrieval system, without permission in writing from the publishers.

Trademark notice: Product or corporate names may be trademarks or registered trademarks, and are used only for identification and explanation without intent to infringe.

British Library Cataloguing-in-Publication Data
A catalogue record for this book is available from the British Library

Library of Congress Cataloging-in-Publication Data
A catalog record has been requested for this book

ISBN: 978-0-367-23700-4 (hbk)
ISBN: 978-0-367-23704-2 (pbk)
ISBN: 978-0-429-28123-5 (ebk)

Typeset in Helvetica & Garamond Three
by Newgen Publishing UK

Printed and bound by CPI Group (UK) Ltd, Croydon, CR0 4YY

This manual is dedicated to all young people who are neuro-diverse, and their friends, family members, teachers, therapists, and community members who support them to imagine, to create, and to belong.

Contents

List of figures and tables   xvi
Foreword   xvii
Acknowledgements   xxi

Chapter 1   Adolescence and social interaction   1

    The purpose and background of "Imagine, Create, Belong"   1
    The importance of social belonging for young people   3
    Neuro-diversity and social difficulties   5
    A different approach for neuro-diverse adolescents   6
    Theoretical underpinnings of "Imagine, Create, Belong"   7
    Application of theory to practice for adolescents in mainstream schools: "Imagine, Create, Belong"   15
    Underlying assumptions of "Imagine, Create, Belong" for adolescents with additional needs   15
    Conclusion   17
    References   18

Chapter 2	**How to use this manual**	**25**

About the programme and who benefits   25
Aims of the programme   26
Additional aims for adolescents who attend a special school   27
About the manual   28
Facilitators   29
The organisation of sessions and activities in Chapters 3–10   30
The activities   32
Preparation for Session 1   35
Conclusion   36
References   37

Chapter 3	**Session 1: Setting the scene**	**39**

What should I expect?   39
Aims of Session 1   40
Theories, abilities, and approaches underpinning Session 1   41
Section A: Suggestions for mainstream school settings   42
Facilitators' toolkit   42
Introductions and session outline   42
Warm up activity   43
Tuning in activity   44
Action activity   45
Closure activity   46
Section B: For adolescents with additional needs   46
Facilitators' toolkit   46
Introduction   47
Warm up activity   47
Tuning in activity   48
Action activity   49
Closure activity   52

| Chapter 4 | Session 2: Participants' life story and the life story of the character | 54 |

What should I expect? 54
Aims of Session 2 55
Theories, abilities, and approaches
  underpinning Session 2 55
**Section A: For mainstream school
  settings** 56
Facilitators' toolkit 56
Introduction 57
Warm up activity 57
Tuning in activity 57
Action activity 59
Closure activity 61
**Section B: For adolescents with
  additional needs** 61
Facilitators' toolkit 61
Introduction 62
Warm up activity 62
Tuning in activity 62
Action activity 64
Closure activity 65
References 66

| Chapter 5 | Session 3: Narrative and identity: How does your character act and feel? | 67 |

What should I expect? 67
Aims of Session 3 68
Theories, abilities, and approaches
  underpinning Session 3 68
**Section A: For mainstream school
  settings** 69
Facilitators' toolkit 69
Introduction 69
Warm up activity 69
Tuning in activity 70

Action activity 72
Closure activity 73
Section B: For adolescents with additional needs 73
Facilitators' toolkit 74
Introduction 74
Warm up activity 74
Tuning in activity 75
Action activity 76
Closure activity 78

Chapter 6   Session 4: Context, plot structure, props, and scenes   80

What should I expect? 80
Aims of Session 4 81
Theories, abilities, and approaches underpinning Session 4 81
Section A: For mainstream school settings 82
Facilitators' toolkit 82
Introduction 82
Warm up activity 82
Tuning in activity 84
Action activity 85
Closure activity 88
Section B: For adolescents with additional needs 88
Facilitators' toolkit 88
Introduction 89
Warm up activity 89
Tuning in activity 89
Action activity 90
Closure activity 91

Chapter 7	Session 5: Beginning to identify problems to solve in the story	93

        What should I expect? 93
        Aims of Session 5 94
        Theories, abilities, and approaches underpinning Session 5 94
        Section A: For mainstream school settings 95
        Facilitators' toolkit 95
        Introduction 95
        Warm up activity 95
        Tuning in activity 96
        Action activity 98
        Closure activity 98
        Section B: Adolescents with additional needs 99
        Facilitators' toolkit 99
        Introduction 99
        Warm up activity 100
        Tuning in activity 100
        Action activity 101
        Closure activity 102
        Reference 113

Chapter 8	Session 6: How will the characters solve the identified problems and what are the props for the movie?	104

        What should I expect? 104
        Aims of Session 6 105
        Theories, abilities, and approaches underpinning Session 6 105
        Section A: For mainstream school settings 106
        Facilitators' toolkit 106

Introduction   106
Warm up activity   107
Tuning in activity   107
Action activity   108
Closure activity   109
Section B: Adolescents with additional needs   110
Facilitators' toolkit   110
Introduction   110
Warm up and tuning in activity   110
Action activity   111
Closure activity   112
Reference   113

Chapter 9   Session 7: Bringing it all together   114

What should I expect?   114
Aims of Session 7   115
Theories, abilities, and approaches underpinning Session 7   115
Section A: For mainstream school settings   116
Facilitators' toolkit   116
Introduction   116
Warm up and tuning in activity   116
Action activity   117
Closure activity   118
Section B: Adolescents with additional needs   118
Facilitators' toolkit   119
Introduction   119
Warm up and tuning in activity   119
Action activity   120
Closure activity   121
Reference   122

Chapter 10	Session 8: The grand finale	123
	What should I expect? 123	
	Aims of Session 8 124	
	Theories, abilities, and approaches underpinning Session 8 124	
	Section A: For mainstream school settings 125	
	Facilitators' toolkit 125	
	Introduction 126	
	Warm up activity and tuning in activity 126	
	Action activity 126	
	Closure activity 127	
	Section B: Adolescents with additional needs 127	
	Facilitators' toolkit 127	
	Introduction 128	
	Warm up and tuning in activity 128	
	Action activity 129	
	Closure activity 129	
Chapter 11	Epilogue	131

Appendix 1: Blank storyboard sheets 133
Appendix 2: Strength cards 134
Appendix 3: Visual schedule 135
Appendix 4: Visual supports 138
Appendix 5: Genogram, ecomap, and Tree of Life 140
Appendix 6: Character cards or choice cards 143
Appendix 7: Goal and problem cards 144
Index 145

List of figures and tables

FIGURES

2.1	Underpinning ability of pretend play for adolescence	28
A1.1	Storyboard example	133
A5.1	Genogram and ecomap	141
A5.2	Tree of Life	142

TABLES

3.1	Tally board	52
A4.1	Chat board example	139
A6.1	Character cards or choice cards	143
A7.1	Goal and problem cards	144

Foreword

In producing the programme "Imagine, Create, Belong", Sophie Goldingay and Karen Stagnitti have provided an innovative and much-needed programme to support the development of social skills in adolescents for whom social interaction is challenging. Successful navigation of social relationships is dependent on abilities such as being able to consider the perspective of another (Hughes & Leekam, 2004), to hold and manipulate abstract concepts in order to sustain the thread of conversation (Baines & Howe, 2010), and to organise our thinking so that we can clearly express our own thoughts and feelings to others (Norrick, 2000). Thus, social communication draws on an intricate interplay of skills and, for some individuals, everyday interactions can become a source of consternation as they try to figure out how to participate in social situations.

The authors make a strong argument for complex pretend play as an integral foundation for successful development of social interaction skills in adolescence. There is a substantial body of literature indicating the importance of play in the early years for increased ability to share information, problem solve, and to engage in sequential thinking (for example, Lillard, 2015). However, as the authors note in Chapter 1, the role of social pretend play with peers in adolescent development has previously received little attention. The principles of "Imagine, Create, Belong" have their basis in theoretical approaches which have been highly influential in shaping our understanding of child development, the role of socio-cultural context, and the importance of person-centred clinical approaches. The recognition of the fundamental impact of play development is the lynchpin of this novel approach to intervening in adolescent social skills through age-appropriate play. The first chapter provides a comprehensive discussion on the interconnection between pretend play, narrative, theory of mind, and social competence, as well as the importance of a positive, person-centred, and collaborative approach to therapy, providing an excellent introduction to the programme.

"Imagine, Create, Belong" is designed for neuro-diverse adolescents, including those who have been diagnosed with Autism Spectrum Disorder (ASD), Attention Deficit Hyperactivity Disorder (ADHD), Post-Traumatic Stress Disorder (PTSD) or dyspraxia, or have a learning disability. However, it can be used with any adolescent who experiences social difficulties. The versatility of the programme is evident in the diverse participants eligible to participate, and the variety of settings in which the programme can be implemented (for example, schools, clinics), as detailed in Chapter 2. The manual also includes an adapted programme for adolescents who have challenging behaviours and intellectual disabilities and who attend special schools. This capacity of the programme to encompass such a breadth of participants is a key strength.

Chapters 3–10 provide detailed session plans for "Imagine, Create, Belong". The eight-session programme is well-structured with a clear statement of aims, and helpful hints to ensure the programme delivery is coherent with the theoretical bases discussed in the opening chapter. A comprehensive description of the role of facilitators, with thoughtful guidance to promote person-centred approaches, is set out in Chapter 2 and woven throughout the manual; there are suggestions for how to support sensory processing needs, as well as calming activities/objects and communication supports, and consideration of cultural diversity. Every chapter clearly sets out session aims, providing plans for mainstream settings (Section A) along with plans for adolescents with additional needs (Section B), with the structure replicated in each session. The flexibility of the programme is evident in the capacity to switch between sections as per the needs of the group, choose from a range of activities, and in the timing of the intervention. The authors stress that the manual provides guidance rather than prescription, and this is manifest throughout the programme. I particularly like that themes can be specifically chosen to reflect the interests of the participants in the group, and that participants are encouraged to draw on their own interests for key elements of the activities, facilitating engagement critical for optimising outcomes. The weekly "action activity" which culminates in making a movie is fun and age-appropriate while simultaneously targeting the core skills outlined in Chapter 1 as integral to developing social abilities. The authors also consider "what next?" for the participants. Chapter 11 provides guidance on how to facilitate ongoing participation in activities that sparked the interest of group members, supporting maintenance of skills and expanding the sense of belonging central to the programme.

Sophie's expertise in identity, well-being, and inclusion for young people in educational settings and correctional facilities, and Karen's extensive knowledge of pretend play development in neuro-typical and neuro-diverse children are combined here to create an outstanding intervention. Pilot studies of the programme have yielded measurable improvements in the ability of the participants to engage in flexible and sequential thinking, to self-regulate, to empathise, and to demonstrate awareness of self as a social being (Goldingay et al., 2015, Goldingay et al., under review). Additionally, anecdotal evidence from the implementation of the adapted programme for adolescents who attend special schools from Donna Davidson and Eleanor Francis indicated similar improvements for participants in these vital social skills.

By developing an intervention for adolescents that is novel in its approach, well-structured, and yet also flexible to enable authentic person-centred delivery, the authors have succeeded in producing a programme that will be of considerable benefit in making a positive difference for adolescents identified as having social difficulties. It is an exciting contribution to a significant area of need, and I have no doubt that it will prove an invaluable asset for clinicians and teachers. I look forward to utilising this programme in my own work.

REFERENCES

Baines, E., & Howe, C. (2010). Discourse topic management and discussion skills in middle childhood: The effects of age and task. *First Language*, 30(3–4), 508–535. https://doi.org/10.1177/0142723710370538

Goldingay, S., Stagnitti, K., Sheppard, L., McGillivray, J., McLean, B., & Pepin, G. (2015). An intervention to improve social participation for adolescents with autism spectrum disorder: Pilot study. *Developmental Neurorehabilitation*, *18*(2), 122–130.

Goldingay, S., Stagnitti, K., Robertson, N., Sheppard, L., Dean, B., & Pepin, G. (under review). Group comparison intervention to facilitate social skills in a group of adolescents.

Hughes, C., & Leekam, S. (2004). What are the links between theory of mind and social links? Review, reflections and new directions for studies of typical and atypical development. *Social Development*, *13*, 590–691. https://doi.org/10.1111/j.1467-9507.2004.00285.x

Lillard, A. (2015). The development of play. In L. S. Liben & U. Mueller (Eds), *Handbook of child psychology and developmental science: Volume 2: Cognitive processes* (pp. 425–468). New York: Wiley-Blackwell.

Norrick, N. R. (2000). *Conversational narrative: Storytelling in everyday talk*. Amsterdam: John Benjamins.

Susan Douglas
PhD (Linguistics), BA (Hons), MSPA, CPSP

Acknowledgements

We acknowledge the Wadawurrung people of the Kulin Nation, Traditional Owners of the land where "Imagine, Create, Belong" was created. We pay our respects to elders past, present, and emerging, and acknowledge Aboriginal and Torres Strait Islander participants and facilitators.

We would also like to acknowledge Associate Professor Genevieve Pepin, Associate Professor Loretta Sheppard, and Professor Jane McGillivray who contributed to the design, data collection, and analysis of the original pilot study for this programme.

CHAPTER 1

Adolescence and social interaction

THE PURPOSE AND BACKGROUND OF "IMAGINE, CREATE, BELONG"

The purpose of the "Imagine, Create, Belong" programme is to facilitate an increased capacity of the young people aged 11–15 years (early to mid-adolescence) to understand and respond appropriately to social situations. Because of this increased social understanding, the young person's world is more cohesive, with an increased shift to a more positive sense of self. "Imagine, Create, Belong" aims to support adolescents who are neuro-diverse. This includes young people with Attention Deficit Hyperactivity Disorder (ADHD), Post-Traumatic Stress Disorder (PTSD), Autism Spectrum Disorder (ASD), and learning and language problems who have social difficulties. "Imagine, Create, Belong" is underpinned by the theoretical foundations of cognitive developmental play theories – particularly pretend play development – and Vygotsky's social constructionist view of development, as well as person-centred therapy based on the work of Carl Rogers and applied to younger people by Virginia Axline.

This approach came about through a serendipitous morning coffee chat between Sophie Goldingay and Karen Stagnitti at their work base university campus at Deakin University. Sophie had completed a doctorate working with young prisoners in New Zealand. She had noticed that often they seemed to have misunderstood the social circumstances of why they were now in prison. Some appeared to have difficulty imagining the impact of their actions on themselves or other people.

This was very different to not caring about what happened – it was clear many cared very deeply. Rather, it was more that some could not imagine it until it was pointed out or they were having a victim's impact statement read out at a criminal trial. Karen had been working in the area of pretend play and had developed several play assessments and a therapy approach for children with developmental issues called "Learn to Play Therapy". Together they pieced together the hypothesis that some of the young people Sophie had worked with in her social work practice and during her doctoral studies possibly had not developed complex pretend play as children and were struggling with concepts of theory of mind, and lacked the ability to anticipate the consequences of their actions and think in sequential ways. Sophie then brought together a research team to create and study an approach based on principles of pretend play and narrative development, developed by Karen, which was suitable for neuro-diverse young people. Belinda Dean and Narelle Robertson were part of the research team and were involved in two studies trialling an eight-session therapeutic intervention that became "Imagine, Create, Belong". Donna Davidson and Eleanor Francis became aware of this approach and could see the possibilities of this programme for young people who attended special school because of their challenging social behaviours, intellectual capacities below an Intelligence Quota (IQ) of 70, and neuro-diversity. Donna and Eleanor have used "Imagine, Create, Belong" with this group of young people and found it to be associated with positive changes in a reduction of challenging behaviours and more social awareness. The adaptations of "Imagine, Create, Belong" made by Donna and Eleanor are in this manual.

This chapter outlines the theoretical underpinnings of "Imagine, Create, Belong". Chapter 2 presents how to use this manual and the specific techniques for facilitators found to be effective within the programme and tied to the theoretical underpinnings. The remaining Chapters 3– 10 are practical and outline each of the eight sessions of "Imagine, Create, Belong", with a chapter for each session. Chapter 11 provides ideas for further developing participants' involvement in more independent ways that do not require facilitators. Within each of these chapters, the adaptations of "Imagine, Create, Belong" for that session for adolescents with more challenging neuro-diversity are presented, after an explanation of the format and activities used within the research studies with adolescents from mainstream high schools who were neuro-diverse. For the adaptations for each session, two sessions are provided by Donna and Eleanor because they found, when working through the programme with adolescents with challenging neuro-diversity, greater repetition and explicit teaching of foundational concepts was required.

THE IMPORTANCE OF SOCIAL BELONGING FOR YOUNG PEOPLE

Adolescence is a period beginning around 12 years of age and continuing into the early 20s (Yasenik & Gardner, 2017). In Western culture, early to mid-adolescence is a time of increased social interaction outside of family, with interpersonal relationships becoming more important (Harter, 2012; Nippold et al., 2014) as the young person strives to separate themselves from parents and differentiate themselves as unique (Harter, 2012). This view of adolescence comes from Western derived stage theories posited by Anna Freud and Erik Erikson in the 1950s and fits Western understandings that the autonomous individual is the basic building block of society (Drewery & Bird, 2004) where the development of personal autonomy and individualism is important. Young people spend more time with peers as opposed to adult family members, navigating social relationships and telling stories about themselves (autobiographical narratives) to achieve a sense of belonging and emotional support (Nippold et al., 2014).

Experiences of young people at this age in cultures not derived from an individualist Western tradition are likely to differ from those cited above, however. For example, collectivist cultures may prioritise deepening connections and relatedness with kin during adolescence as opposed to separation from them. In New Zealand, Mason Durie (1998) notes for Maori that identity development is a collectivist process to deepen family connections across the generations, both past and present. In Australia, young people of Aboriginal and Torres Strait Island nations are also likely to experience the process of healthy growing to maturity differently. Identity for Aboriginal people comes with oral sharing of the history, stories of their bloodline that connect them to their traditional land, beliefs and values. Thus, identity, connection to culture, and community become of interest at this age but can also be challenging (Eccles 2019, personal communication). A research project in Melbourne, based on a partnership with a local Aboriginal Community Controlled organisation which included four senior Aboriginal women as project advisors (Priest, Mackean, Davis, Briggs, & Waters, 2012), found that strong culture was the central core of Aboriginal child health, well-being, and identity development. From interviews with Aboriginal grandparents, parents, aunties, or uncles of Aboriginal children, the researchers found this concept included "passing of cultural knowledge from one generation to the next and modeling of community and gender-related roles" (Priest et al., 2012, p. 184). Thus, rather than aiming for separation and differentiation from parents or parental figures, the process of healthy identity development for Koori (e.g. those who are from Victoria and New South Wales, Australia) adolescents involves spending more time with elders and building connections through participation in community events and ceremony which involves the whole family. A deepening of spiritual connection to Country, with its associated custodian responsibilities, is also an essential part of identity development for Aboriginal and Torres Strait Islander adolescents. Development of storytelling and narrative ability is key to identity development in adolescents irrespective of cultural background, however.

Physically, adolescence is also a period of major brain re-organisation and pruning (Siegel & Bryson, 2012; Siegel, 2012, 2013), with the highest volume of grey matter in the brain occurring during early adolescence (Yasenik & Gardner, 2017, p. 74). The brain's capacity to process emotions is "fully online" but with control of emotional impulses still maturing (Yasenik & Gardner, 2017, p. 74). Prior to adolescence, the autobiographical memory of a 10-year-old young person is in their control as they become the owner of their own story, with the ability to evaluate what others think of them while becoming more concerned about what others think of them. In this pre-adolescent time, older children use social comparisons for assessments of their personal competence, alongside being able to describe themselves by characteristics (Harter, 2012). For some young people, adolescence sees a dramatic increase in social awareness and self-consciousness of others' opinions (particularly peers) of who they are (Harter, 2012). As noted for both Western and non-Western adolescents, significant adults are important during the period of mid-adolescence, as they support the young person's autobiographical account of past, present, and future.

During early adolescence, young people are changing in their language and cognitive abilities. They are moving from concrete to formal operational thought, and this makes it possible for them "to engage in hypothetical-deductive reasoning, the ability to think logically and abstractly about complex issues" (Nippold et al., 2014, p. 878). Young adolescents may begin to show interest in discussion of social, political, or religious topics and, as they are very aware of hypocrisy in others, may do so from an idealistic perspective (Harter, 2012; Nippold et al., 2014). Changes in their cognitive capacities are shown in an increasing ability to take a socially oriented perspective, that is, what is good for society, more than a perspective primarily centred on the self (Nippold et al., 2014). They use longer sentences to express themselves with narratives that show more complex language structures (Nippold et al., 2014). Oral language competence, including narrative competence, underpins literacy achievements and contributes to academic achievement (Nicolopoulou, Barbosa de Sá, Ilgaz, & Brockmeyer, 2010; Snow & Powell, 2011).

NEURO-DIVERSITY AND SOCIAL DIFFICULTIES

Adolescence, then, is a time of major change for the young person – in brain development, sense of self, and cognitive and language capacities. For some adolescents who are neuro-diverse and who struggle with social situations, their experience may be more of loneliness and rejection which, in turn, increases anxiety levels and compounds their social difficulties (Parker & Asher, 1987). Young people who are neuro-diverse may have greater difficulty coping with complex social situations in adolescence and may find themselves isolated, which contributes to poorer well-being (Parker & Asher, 1987). Social difficulties have been related to lower oral language and narrative abilities. Snow and Powell (2011) found that young offenders had lower oral language ability than expected for age (which supports Sophie

Goldingay's observations during her practice experience and doctoral studies). Oral language also includes telling stories, and an ability to tell a narrative coherently has been reported as being difficult for children with autism (Stirling, Douglas, Leekam, & Carey, 2014). For young people aged 10–12 years with ASD and co-morbid ADHD symptoms, executive function difficulties were associated with ADHD symptoms, with associations between executive function and theory of mind impairments also providing insight into the functioning of these young people (Lukito et al., 2017). "Imagine, Create, Belong" was developed with these young people as the focus of this programme.

A DIFFERENT APPROACH FOR NEURO-DIVERSE ADOLESCENTS

Approaches such as Cognitive Behavioural Therapy through to social skill development and emotional insight may be ineffective for neuro-diverse young people due to problems with attention, language, and memory (Goldingay & Stagnitti, 2014). Approaches such as Cognitive Behavioural Therapy require insight and cognitive capacities with the linking of feelings and behaviours that many young neuro-diverse people struggle with (Attwood & Scarpa, 2013). In adolescence, many young people who are neuro-diverse have experienced developmental difficulties as they have grown up, such as: reduced ability to read social situations; lack of understanding of social contexts; poorer ability to negotiate with peers; lack of narrative ability, including difficulty extending a story, identifying and resolving problems in the story, poorer understanding of characters' emotions, actions, and what they would say; and following conversations (related to logical sequential thought processes). These difficulties are also present in children with poor pretend play ability (Stagnitti, 2016a; Stagnitti & Unsworth, 2000). Goldingay et al. (2015) found that neuro-diverse young people show deficits in pretend play ability, particularly the link between creating a story (narrative) and play. Studies have found that embodiment of the story in role play ("embodiment", also being called "embodied cognition", that is, the whole body is moved to act out the story) is more effective for recall of the story than just using a puppet, play props, or pictures (Lillard et al., 2013). This shows that the deeper the physical and emotional engagement in the play, the more likely the child is to engage in a cohesive narrative, thus developing this ability for use later in life. In addition, Gray (2011) found a correlation between increased play in childhood and decreased anxiety and depression in adolescence.

An age-appropriate play-based approach, then, offers an alternative to working with adolescents who are neuro-diverse and who experience difficulties in social settings. Many young people with developmental difficulties have not developed foundational skills through early play behaviour and during early play behaviour were often not involved in group play to a complex level of playing a scenario over several days or weeks with peers. Hence, while some young people who are neuro-diverse with ASD can engage in pretend play (Chaudry & Dissanayake, 2016), the complexity and length of playing may not match that of their peers. Thus, skills, such as awareness of the thoughts and mental states of others (theory of mind) and ability to think in sequential ways for developing and understanding a cohesive narrative that evolves in the play, may not be developed.

THEORETICAL UNDERPINNINGS OF "IMAGINE, CREATE, BELONG"

Several theoretical approaches influenced the development and design of "Imagine, Create, Belong". This section explains these approaches, starting with early pretend play development and links to social competence, narrative, theory of mind, and representational thinking. Next, social constructivism, as put forward by Vygotsky, is explained followed by person-centred therapy, which was originally articulated by Rogers. All these influences are then distilled into the principles that underpin "Imagine, Create, Belong".

Pretend play, social ability, narrative, and theory of mind

The importance of complex pretend play in early and middle childhood as a foundation for function and further development in adolescence is often overlooked or dismissed. Pretend play is the type of play where children impose meaning beyond who they are, the literal props that they have, or the space they are playing in. For example, if children are playing "outer space", the box "becomes" a rocket and the space they are playing in "becomes" the solar system, and they themselves become astronauts. The children have gone beyond the literality of what and where they are playing. This type of play was put forward as developing in an inverted U-shaped function (Fein, 1981; Piaget, 1962), where changes in pretend play peak in the preschool years and then other forms of play take its place. Hence, pretend play was interpreted as not being relevant to adolescence. This view has been challenged. In 2005, Göncü and Perone argued that pretend play was a life-span activity and was "an adaptive human activity of adulthood as well as childhood" (p. 137). Brown and Vaughan (2009) argued strongly that play in childhood is an essential element that contributes to well-being in adulthood and that adults still need to play for their own well-being.

It is an assumption underpinning "Imagine, Create, Belong" that play does change form as children develop (Gaskill & Perry, 2014), and that pretend play changes form, from the young child playing with peers in pretend scenarios to "being a mental process that informs social communication" in adolescence (Stagnitti, 2017, p. 188). Early complex social pretend play behaviour requires "sustained reciprocal dialogue and reciprocal action between peers" which place greater intellectual demands on children (Whitebread & O'Sullivan, 2012, p. 200). These early experiences with peers build skills in relation to: understanding context; reading social situations; understanding what characters say, do, and how they act during a play scene; ability to extend and build on a story, add problems to the story to resolve, negotiate with others, and talk through the story as it is being carried out. Goldingay et al. (2015) found that adolescents who were neurodiverse had difficulty in social interactions with peers to build a cohesive storyline as a group. On an early version of the Animated Movie Test (Goldingay et al., 2015; Stagnitti, 2018), they had difficulty initiating ideas, sequencing a story, generating problems, and embedding character roles in the story.

Pretend play is connected with narrative, social competence, and theory of mind (Stagnitti, 2016a). In childhood, the development of narrative ability parallels pretend play development (Stagnitti & Jellie, 2006). In adolescence, Nippold et al. (2014) aligned competent ability in narrative with social, academic, and practical everyday functions because competent narrative requires "the ability to remember events, organise information, understand the epistemological and emotional perspectives of others, and employ complex syntax and appropriate vocabulary to express oneself with clarity, precision, and efficiency" (p. 876). Ability in narrative involves being able to understand character motivations, sequential thought, cause-effect thinking to resolve a problem, and using temporal sequencing. Ability in narrative is also important for sense of self as adolescents build their own autobiographical memories and tell other stories about themselves to build social relationships and friendship groups (Harter, 2012; Nippold et al., 2014). This correlation between storytelling ability and identity is also written about by Aboriginal writers in the East and South Eastern regions of Australia. For example, from a Gumbaynggirr perspective, Michael Donovan notes that "the use of story is present through all aspects of the lives of Indigenous peoples, including Aboriginal people, and has been used as a major learning and information tool" (2015, p.616). Writing from a D'harawal perspective, Bodkin writes, "storytelling is one of our most important methods of communication, learning and promoting mutual respect and understanding" (as cited in Bodkin-Andrews, Bodkin, Andrews, & Evans (2017, p. 29)). In Geelong, where "Imagine, Create, Belong" originated, Glen Shea created a game for adolescents called *The Storyteller* (Shea, 2012), described as an educational tool for young people to provide cultural knowledge and aid understanding. Other tools to build a story of self and collective identity from an Aboriginal perspective include the "Tree of Life" by Wadawurrung Traditional Owner Corrina Eccles (Eccles, 2019 personal communication) (see Appendix 5 of this manual).

Pretend play includes the use of symbols in play. Symbols in play can be, for example, using a container as a building. Symbols in play is called "object substitution" in this manual. Object substitution has been found to be associated with social competence and participation in pre-adolescence (Roberts, Stagnitti, Brown, & Bhopti, 2018; Uren & Stagnitti, 2009). The link between using symbols in play and social participation is not immediately obvious. Karen Stagnitti has speculated that the ability to use symbols in play utilises abstract conceptualisations in thought and social competence requires multiple facets of skills, such as taking into account verbal and non-verbal communication and reading a context, so both abilities require the ability of representational thinking.

Reading a social context requires theory of mind. Theory of mind begins to develop as early as 18 months old (Baron-Cohen, 1996) and many researchers note that the emergence of theory of mind coincides with pretend play development (Hughes & Leekam, 2004). Further studies investigating theory of mind ability within typically developing samples have explored the impact of shared environment (for example, interactions with siblings), verbal ability, socio-economic status, and genetics (for example, twin studies) (Hughes et al., 2005). One view put forward is an interaction between nature and nurture where innate mechanisms influence early milestones in theory of mind (such as joint attention, imitation) and social environments influence later development in theory in mind (such as representational mental states) (Hughes et al., 2005). Theory of mind research has identified key moments of development, such as the first-order false-belief task of recursive thinking (that is, I think that you think), which has been observed from 4 years of age; and the second-order false-belief task of recursive thinking (that is, I think that you think that he/she thinks), which has been observed at 8 years of age (Valle, Massaro, Castelli, & Marchetti, 2015, p. 112). Adolescence, with major changes in brain development, cognitive, narrative, and social areas, requires an increase in ability in theory of mind as adolescents understand their own and others' minds (Valle et al., 2015). A third level of recursive thinking is "I think that you think that he/she thinks that another person thinks…" (Valle et al., 2015, p. 114). Valle and colleagues carried out a study where they explored how adolescents performed on two theory of mind tasks. One task was to recognise the correct mental state of a character and the second task was to attribute the correct mental state to predict the character's behaviour (Valle et al., 2015). In their study there were 47 fourteen-year-olds, 43 seventeen-year-olds, and 20 twenty-year-old young people. They found that the third level of recursive thinking was difficult for fourteen-year-olds, with twenty-year-olds being significantly better at the task than young adolescents (Valle et al., 2015). Hence, Valle et al. showed the continuing development of theory of mind ability from adolescence to early adulthood. Theory of mind is linked to narrative because understanding motives and perspectives of characters are required for both tasks (Snow, Powell, & Sanger, 2012; Stagnitti, 2016a). Neuro-diverse young people have been reported to have poorer skills in theory of mind than same aged peers and may have unique language profiles including impaired semantic and pragmatic language abilities (Attwood & Scarpa, 2013).

Social constructivism

The social constructivism model, which stemmed from the views of Vygotsky, emphasises the socio-cultural context in learning (Mallory & New, 1994). Vygotsky put forward that a better understanding of the dynamics of a young person's intellectual progress was not a measure of mental age but rather how the young person solved problems in collaboration with capable peers and adults (Vygotsky, 1934/1986). He called this the "zone of proximal development" (Vygotsky, 1934/1986, p. 187). Vygotsky's understanding of developmental changes is also relevant to "Imagine, Create, Belong" because he viewed development as resembling the geological structure of the earth's core (Vygotsky, 1934/1986, p. xxix) with differentiated layers. Applied to his developmental approach, lower stages of development are superseded by higher stages, however lower stages do not disappear. How a young person understood a concept at a particular time was reliant on how many "geological layers" it was in and which role it played, depending on the "layer" that was activated (Vygotsky, 1934/1986, p. xxix). As "Imagine, Create, Belong" is rooted in building complex concepts from pretend play, such as representational thought, logical sequential thought, object substitution, and ability to decentre from the self and impose meaning on something or someone outside of the self, young people come to the programme with layers of already established skill. Through the facilitators working with the young people, creating a "zone of proximal development", the skills of the young people are further developed so that they can engage more complex concepts, which may not have been mastered previously. Thus, "Imagine, Create, Belong" builds on what participants are already familiar with in order to promote their development. The young people are not passive participants but rather "make meaning of the world through their interactions" while they also modify and transform the materials, storyline, and people in their environment (Martinez, Dye, & Gonzalez, 2017, p. 514).

Person-centred therapy

The third influence underpinning "Imagine, Create, Belong" is person-centred therapy. Person-centred therapy was originally developed by Carl Rogers in the 1940s as client-centred therapy (Meador & Rogers, 1973). The central hypothesis was "that the growthful potential of any individual will tend to be released in a relationship in which the helping person is experiencing and communicating realness, caring and a deeply sensitive non-judgemental understanding" (Meador & Rogers, 1973, p. 119). Rogers developed the process-oriented person-centred therapy for adults in the context of an interview between the client and therapist. Virginia Axline, a student of Rogers, went on to develop non-directive play therapy for children (Axline, 1974). In Axline's approach, toys, play props, and art works are the medium of the therapy. On a continuum of interview to play materials as the context for the process of person-centred therapy, "Imagine, Create, Belong" sits closer to Axline's approach where props and art materials are the medium for the therapeutic intervention.

The basic theory of client-centred therapy can be stated as the "if-then" hypothesis: "if certain conditions are present in the attitudes of the person designated as 'therapist' in a relationship, namely congruence, positive regard, and empathic understanding, then growthful change will take place in the 'other,' the person designated 'client'" (Meador & Rogers, 1973, pp.125–126). Congruence, positive regard, and empathic understanding are articulated into the following principles for the facilitators of "Imagine, Create, Belong". These principles are also influenced by Axline's eight basic principles (Axline, 1974, p.73–74).

1. The therapeutic relationship must be engaging and inviting, providing warmth and rapport at the earliest possible moment.
2. The young person must be unconditionally accepted by the therapist.
3. The therapeutic environment must be non-judgemental in order for the young person to feel uninhibited in the expression of emotions, feelings, and behaviours.
4. The therapist must be attentive and cognisant of the young person's behaviours in order to provide empathic reflective comments verbally and non-verbally back to the young person so that he or she may develop self-awareness.
5. The therapist relies on the young person's ability to find solutions, when available, to his or her own problems and understands that the young person is solely responsible for the transformational choices he or she makes or does not make.
6. The therapist acts as the shadow, allowing the child to lead the therapeutic journey through dialogue and actions.
7. The therapist recognises that the procedure is one that is steady and should progress at its own pace, not a pace set by the therapist.
8. The only limitations and boundaries that are set are ones that ensure the therapeutic process stays genuine and that the young person remains in the realm of reality, aware of his or her purpose and role in the therapy.

Through these principles of person-centred therapy, the key purpose of the beginning session of "Imagine, Create, Belong" is to establish a non-judgemental therapeutic environment that builds on participants' strengths and supports engagement in the activities at their own pace. The young person is accepted as they are when they come into the sessions. For some young people, their presentation may vary from session to session, depending on socio-cultural events during the intervening time between sessions. Irrespective of how participants present, processes that support rapport and relationship building that are inviting, age-appropriate and warm are essential.

Rapport building may be further supported through mutual sharing of interests and being attentive to the meanings behind participants' behaviours (for example, if a participant feels uncomfortable with direct questions, finding more circular ways of encouraging conversation). Unconditional acceptance of challenges faced by participants is key. In addition, inviting participants to bring an item they like from home may further scaffold interaction in the group (we call this "neuro-responsive social scaffolding"). Such items may include electronic devices, which support neuro-diverse adolescents to share what they are interested in and good at with others, and to retreat from social interaction and "recharge" if the social situation starts to become overwhelming. Being able to do this enables them to stay connected and included in the group and participate at their own pace. Also important is the notion that a participant can choose to participate in the activity, and that if they choose not to, alternative activities which build on their strengths may be used instead. Flexibility is essential.

The creation of an environment of acceptance and engagement with "Imagine, Create, Belong" includes activities of known age-appropriate discussion and engagement prompts. For instance, in the practical chapters that follow, examples of popular animated children's movies or games are suggested to be used to scaffold participation in the group. These activities are suggested so participants who struggle in group settings can join in the activity without awkwardness. Ideas include Minecraft™ or other interactive collaborative online games that are appreciated by boys or girls, the *Lego*™ *Movie*, or Mario Kart. (At the time of writing, these games/activities were current and are given as an example of age-appropriate activities.)

This manual gives a structure and ideas for each session; however, it is important to be willing to adapt each week according to how the group is progressing. This is embedded within the principles of person-centred therapy. The young people need to be met in a way that suits them without judgement.

APPLICATION OF THEORY TO PRACTICE FOR ADOLESCENTS IN MAINSTREAM SCHOOLS: "IMAGINE, CREATE, BELONG"

Neuro-responsive social scaffolding is a phrase used in the "Imagine, Create, Belong" programme and is defined as: responding to neuro-divergence by scaffolding social interactions alongside use of supportive objects or calming activities. Scaffolding skills in a progressive way comes from the constructivist ideas in the work of Vygotsky, with the person-centred principles based on Rogers' work. When applied to scaffolding social skills in a weekly programme for neuro-divergent young people, it means the expectations and sociability of the activities are gradually increased over the course of the 8 weeks with the use of props of their choosing (the zone of proximal development). These may include electronic devices, stress balls, or other items. This supports the young people to engage at their own pace (person-centred principle).

Supporting participants to create something new from what they have learnt (constructive activity) and then explain it to their peers (interactive activity) leads to deep learning and metacognitive engagement in the task (Chi, 2009). This approach in "Imagine, Create, Belong" brings together the zones of proximal development with both facilitator and peers, while responding to the young person in building complex pretend play and increasing representational thinking.

When working with neuro-diverse young people, repetition is important, and this is reflected in the eight-week programme, which focuses on character and story development. Repetition with variation (Stagnitti, 2016b) is a feature of Learn to Play Therapy and has been found to be a critical therapeutic skill in extending the cognitive and social abilities of participants. Repetition with variation is also embedded in the practicalities of responding to young people to build their capabilities.

UNDERLYING ASSUMPTIONS OF "IMAGINE, CREATE, BELONG" FOR ADOLESCENTS WITH ADDITIONAL NEEDS

Donna Davidson and Eleanor Francis trialled "Imagine, Create, Belong" at a special developmental school in Melbourne, Victoria,

Australia. An adapted programme was developed to support this cohort to access the content within the original "Imagine, Create, Belong" programme over 16 sessions. The adapted programme has been run with seven groups since 2016. Participants in this programme have been aged 8–18, all had an IQ under 55, and many of these participants had Complex Communication Needs (CCN). The underlying assumptions for adolescents with developmental difficulties are similar to the underlying assumptions of "Imagine, Create, Belong" with adolescents in mainstream schools who are neuro-diverse. With reference to adolescents with developmental difficulties, the underlying assumptions of "Imagine, Create, Belong" are as follows.

1. Traditional approaches to social skill development may be ineffective for neuro-diverse young people due to problems with attention, language, and memory. Students with a diagnosed intellectual disability often present with associated language disorders, including receptive, expressive, and social difficulties. Additional resources should be implemented to scaffold participants' learning and engagement with the presented material.

2. Early play behaviour is complex and children build skills during this time in relation to: understanding context; reading social situations; understanding what characters say, do, and act during a play scene; ability to extend and build on a story for up to 3 weeks, add problems to the story to resolve, negotiate with others, and talk through the story as it is being carried out.

3. Many neuro-diverse young people have not developed foundational skills through early play behaviour and during early play behaviour were often not involved in group play to a complex level of playing a scenario over several days or weeks with peers.

4. In adolescence, many neuro-diverse young people have a poorer ability to read social situations, understand social contexts, cannot extend stories and include problems in the narrative, have poorer understanding of characters' emotions, actions, and what they would say, have poorer ability to negotiate and have conversations (related to logical sequential thought processes). Impairment in

narrative/oral language ability has been linked to a higher incidence of involvement in the youth justice system as identified by a study of victims of maltreatment (abuse and/or neglect) and young offenders (Snow & Powell, 2005, 2011). Reporting an event in sequence is a very complicated manoeuvre, requiring the child to hold in mind the present time, then to move back (or forward) to the beginning of a prior event, move forward again through the event and reach the end, then move forward to the present (Westby, 1982).

5. The link between impairment in narrative/oral ability and impairments in sequential or consequential thinking is not recognised and young people, as described in 3 and 4 above, appear to have poorer skills or skills at a much younger level than same aged peers. Problems in this area can lead to risky or dangerous behaviour, impacting on the self and others.

6. Effective intervention should meet these young people at their level which is proposed to be significantly lower than same aged peers (According to Abilities Based Learning & Education Support (ABLES) Speaking and Listening assessment; Department of Education and Early Childhood Development, 2011).

7. Adolescents with additional needs may not have learnt fundamental skills underlying integral concepts such as self and other awareness.

8. Repetition is important. Repetition with variation will extend the cognitive and social abilities of participants.

CONCLUSION

This chapter has set out how "Imagine, Create, Belong" came about and the theoretical underpinnings of the programme and the approach. Two research projects, to date, have found that young people who are neuro-diverse enjoy the programme, are motivated to attend (depending on their life circumstances), and grow in empathy, social understanding, narrative or storytelling ability, and representational thought. Development of empathy, which has been noted to increase

(Goldingay et al., 2015), we hypothesise as coming from an increase in the young person's theory of mind, since in "Imagine, Create, Belong" the young person creates a character and gives it attributes, feelings, and thoughts which are different to the self. Supporting activities, such as false-belief tasks, are also included, as this requires the participant to take the perspective of another and to answer questions based on what the other person knows. The activities in the programme are aimed at building complex pretend play which, in turn, is argued to impact on logical sequential thinking, narrative, or storytelling ability and theory of mind. The approach of "Imagine, Create, Belong" is underpinned by the social constructivist model from Vygotsky together with a person-centred approach based on Rogers and Axline.

The next chapter will give more detail on how to use this manual and how to run the programme in different settings. Chapters 3–10 are practical chapters which provide the "how" of the "Imagine, Create, Belong".

REFERENCES

Attwood, T., & Scarpa, A. (2013). Modifications of cognitive-behavioral therapy for children and adolescents with high-functioning ASD and their common difficulties. In A. Scarpa, S. Williams White, & T. Attwood (Eds), *CBT for children and adolescents with high-functioning autism spectrum disorders* (pp. 27–44). New York: Guilford Publications.

Axline, V. (1974). *Play therapy.* New York: Ballantine Books.

Baron-Cohen, S. (1996). *Mindblindness. An essay on autism and theory of mind.* London: The MIT Press.

Bodkin-Andrews, G., Bodkin, F., Andrews, G., & Evans, R. (2017). Aboriginal identity, world views, research and the story of the Burra'gorang. In C. Kickett-Tucker, D. Bessarab, J. Coffin, & M. Wright (Eds), *Mia Mia Aboriginal community development: Fostering cultural security* (pp. 19–36). Cambridge University Press.

Brown, S., & Vaughan, C. (2009). *Play. How it shapes the brain, opens the imagination, and invigorates the soul*. Melbourne: Scribe Publications.

Chaudry, M., & Dissanayake, C. (2016). Pretend play in children with autism spectrum disorders. In S. Douglas & L. Stirling (Eds), *Children's play, pretense, and story: Studies in culture, context, and autism spectrum disorder* (pp. 31–50). New York: Psychology Press.

Chi, M. T. H. (2009). Active-constructive-interactive: A conceptual framework for differentiating learning activities. *Topics in Cognitive Science*, *1*(1), 73–105. doi:10.1111/j.1756-8765.2008.01005.x

Department of Education and Early Childhood Development (2011). *Abilities Based Learning & Education Support: An introductory guide for Victorian Government Schools*. Melbourne: Student Wellbeing Division, Department of Education and Early Childhood Development. Retrieved from www.education.vic.gov.au/Documents/school/teachers/teachingresources/diversity/ablesintroguide.pdf

Donovan, M. J. (2015). Aboriginal student stories, the missing voice to guide us towards change. *The Australian Educational Researcher*, *42*(5): 613–625. https://doi.org/10.1007/s13384-015-0182-3

Drewery, W., & Bird, L. (2004). *Human development in Aotearoa: A journey through life*. Auckland: McGraw-Hill.

Durie, M. (1998). *Whaiora: Maori health development* (2nd ed.). Auckland: Oxford University Press.

Fein, G. (1981). Pretend play in childhood: An integrative review. *Child Development*, *52*, 1095–1118.

Gaskill, R., & Perry, B. D. (2014). The neurobiological power of play: Using the neurosequential model of therapeutics to guide play in the healing process. In C. Malchiodi & D. A Crenshaw (Eds), *Play and creative arts therapy for attachment trauma* (pp. 178–194). New York: Guilford Press.

Goldingay, S., & Stagnitti, K. (2014). Inclusive service design for young people with learning disabilities who exhibit behaviours of concern. In A. Taket, B. Crisp, M. Graham, L. Hanna, S. Goldingay, & L. Wilson (Eds), *Practising social inclusion* (pp. 106–114). London: Routledge.

Goldingay, S., Stagnitti, K., Sheppard, L., McGillivray, J., McLean, B., & Pepin, G. (2015). An intervention to improve social participation for adolescents with autism spectrum disorder: Pilot study. *Developmental Neurorehabilitation*, *18*(2), 122–130. doi:10.3109/17518423.2013.855275

Göncü, A., & Perone, A. (2005). Pretend play as a life-span activity. *Topoi*, *24*, 137–147.

Gray, P. (2011). The decline of play and rise of psychopathology in children and adolescents. *American Journal of Play*, *3*, 443–463.

Harter, S. (2012). *The construction of the self. Developmental and sociocultural foundations* (2nd ed.). New York: The Guildford Press.

Hughes, C., Jaffee, S. R., Happe, F., Taylor, A., Caspi, A., & Moffitt, T. E. (2005). Origins of individual differences in theory of mind: From nature or nurture? *Child Development*, *76*, 356–370.

Hughes, C., & Leekam, S. (2004). What are the links between theory of mind and social links? Review, reflections and new directions for studies of typical and atypical development. *Social Development*, *13*, 590–691.

Lillard, A., Lerner, M., Hopkins, E., Dore, R., Smith, E., & Palmquist, C. (2013). The impact of pretend play on children's development: A review of the evidence. *Psychological Bulletin*, *139*(1), 1–34.

Lukito, S., Jones, C. R. G., Pickles, A., Baird, G., Happe, F., Charman, T., & Simonoff, E. (2017). Specificity of executive function and theory of mind performance in relation to attention-deficit/hyperactivity symptoms in autism spectrum disorders. *Molecular Autism*, e1–13. doi10.1186/s13229-017-0177-1

Mallory, B. L., & New, R. S. (1994). Social constructivist theory and principles of inclusion: Challenges for early childhood special education. *Journal of Special Education*, 28, 322–337.

Martinez, R. R., Dye, L., & Gonzalez, L. M. (2017). A social constructivist approach to preparing school counsellors to work effectively in urban schools. *Urban Review*, 49, 511–528. doi: 10.1007/sl1256-017-0406-0

Meador, B. D., & Rogers, C. R. (1973). Client-centered therapy. In R. Corsini (Ed.), *Current Psychotherapies* (pp.119–165). Illinois: Peacock Publishers.

Nicolopoulou, A., Barbosa de Sá, A., Ilgaz, H., & Brockmeyer, C. (2010). Using the transformative power of play to educate hearts and minds: From Vygotsky to Vivian Paley and beyond. *Mind, Culture and Activity*, 17, 42–58.

Nippold, M. A., Frantz-Kaspar, M. W., Cramond, P. M., Kirk, C., Hayward-Mayhew, C., & MacKinnon, M. (2014). Conversational and narrative speaking in adolescents: Examining the use of complex syntax. *Journal of Speech, Language, and Hearing Research*, 57, 876–886.

Parker, J. G., & Asher, S. R. (1987). Peer relations and later personal adjustment: Are low-accepted children at risk? *Psychological Bulletin*, 102(3), 357–389. doi:10.1037/0033-2909.102.3.357

Piaget, J. (1962). *Play, dreams and imitation in childhood*. (Trans. G. Gattegno and F. M. Hodgson). New York: W. W. Norton & Company.

Priest, N., Mackean, T., Davis, E., Briggs, L., & Waters, E. (2012). Aboriginal perspectives of child health and wellbeing in an urban setting: Developing a conceptual framework. *Health Sociology Review, 21*(2), 180–195. doi:10.5172/hesr.2012.21.180

Roberts, T., Stagnitti, K., Brown, T., & Bhopti, A. (2018). Relationship between sensory processing and pretend play in typically developing children. *American Journal of Occupational Therapy, 72,* p. 1–8.

Shea, G. (2012). *What does The Storyteller Board Game aim to do?* Retrieved from www.djillong.net.au/images/THE_STORYTELLER_leaflet_2012.pdf

Siegel, D. (2012). *The developing mind. How relationships and the brain interact to shape who we are* (2nd ed.). New York: The Guilford Press.

Siegel, D. (2013). *Brainstorm. The power and purpose of the teenage brain.* New York: Penguin.

Siegel, D., & Bryson, T. (2012). *The whole brain child. 12 revolutionary strategies to nurture your child's developing mind.* New York: Bantam Books Trade Paperbacks.

Snow, P. C., & Powell, M. B. (2005). What's the story? An exploration of narrative language abilities in male juvenile offenders. *Psychology, Crime & Law, 11,* 239–253.

Snow, P. C., & Powell, M. B. (2011). Oral language competence in incarcerated young offenders: Links with offending severity. *International Journal of Speech-Language Pathology, 13,* 480–489.

Snow, P. C., Powell, M. B., & Sanger, D. D. (2012). Oral language competence, young speakers, and the law. *Language Speech Hearing Services in Schools, 43*(4), 496–506. doi: 10.1044/0161-1461(2012/11–0065)

Stagnitti, K. (2016a). Play, narrative, and children with Autism. In S. Douglas & L. Stirling (Eds), *Children's play, pretense, and story: Studies in culture, context, and autism spectrum disorder* (pp. 51–71). New York: Psychology Press.

Stagnitti, K. (2016b). Play therapy for school-age children with high functioning autism. In A. Drewes and C. Schaefer (Eds), *Play therapy in middle childhood* (pp. 237–255). New York: American Psychological Association.

Stagnitti, K. (2017). A growing brain – a growing imagination. In E. Prendiville and J. Howard (Eds), *Creative psychotherapy. Applying the principles of neurobiology to play and expressive arts-based practice* (pp. 183–200). London: Routledge.

Stagnitti, K. (2018). *Animated movie test*: Melbourne: Learn to Play.

Stagnitti, K., & Jellie, L. (2006). *Play to learn. Building literacy skills through play*. Melbourne: Curriculum Corporation.

Stagnitti, K., & Unsworth, C. (2000). The importance of pretend play in child development: An occupational therapy perspective. *British Journal of Occupational Therapy*, 63(3), 121–127. http://dx.doi.org/10.1177/030802260006300306

Stirling, L., Douglas, S., Leekam, S., & Carey, L. (2014). The use of narrative in studying communication in autism spectrum disorders. In J. Arciuli and J. Brock (Eds), *Communication in autism* (pp. 171–215). New York: Benjamins.

Uren, N., & Stagnitti, K. (2009). Pretend play, social competence and learning in preschool children. *Australian Occupational Therapy Journal*, 56, 33–40.

Valle, A., Massaro, D., Castelli, I., & Marchetti, A. (2015). Theory of mind development in adolescence and early adulthood: The growing complexity of recursive thinking ability. *Europe's Journal of Psychology*, 11, 112–124.

Vygotsky, L. (1934/1986). *Thought and language*. (Trans. and edited by Alex Kozulin). London: MIT Press.

Westby, C. (1982). Cognitive and linguistic aspects of children's narrative development. *Communication Disorders*, 7, 1–16.

Whitebread, D., & O'Sullivan, L. (2012). Preschool children's social pretend play: Supporting the development of metacommunication, metacognition and self-regulation. *International Journal of Play*, 1, 197–213.

Yasenik, L., & Gardner, K. (2017). Counselling skills in action with children, adolescents, and adults. In E. Prendiville and J. Howard (Eds), *Creative psychotherapy. Applying the principles of neurobiology to play and expressive arts-based practice* (pp. 59–80). London: Routledge.

CHAPTER 2

How to use this manual

ABOUT THE PROGRAMME AND WHO BENEFITS

"Imagine, Create, Belong" is an eight-session programme for small groups of adolescents aged 11–15 years who have been identified by their teachers as having social difficulties. "Imagine, Create, Belong" was designed for young people in their early to mid-adolescence who are neuro-diverse and who may or may not have a formal diagnosis of Autism Spectrum Disorder (ASD), Attention Deficit Hyperactivity Disorder (ADHD), Post-Traumatic Stress Disorder (PTSD) or dyspraxia, or have a learning disability or other condition of neuro-diversity. Sessions may run for 45–60 minutes, depending on the ability and age of participants. For those who are interested in running further sessions, extension activities for a further 4 weeks are provided in Chapter 11.

"Imagine, Create, Belong" has been adapted for adolescents who attend special schools and have challenging behaviours and intellectual disabilities. These adolescents may also be neuro-diverse. This manual includes adaptations for this group of adolescents, with an extension to each of the eight sessions of further repetition for consolidation of skill uptake. The programme can be run in mainstream or special schools as well as clinic settings.

The core activities within "Imagine, Create, Belong" are for the small group of adolescents to form a cohesive narrative around a movie plot. The group decides on what the movie will be, who the characters will be, the narrative of the movie (logical sequential thought), including plot development, problem generation, and resolution. Alongside these core activities, activities for engagement, theory of mind, and representational thought (for example, object substitution) are incorporated into the programme. The activities target complex pretend play ability as a foundation for emotional engagement and further development in social and narrative understanding in adolescents who are neuro-diverse (see Figure 2.1).

The adapted programme (Section B) supports participants to work together while explicitly learning the concepts outlined in the original programme. Additional elements to support understanding of foundational skills, such as physical characteristics and simple story structure, were required in the adapted programme. At the conclusion of the 16-session programme, each participant will have written and produced their own characters and movie. Adaptations have been made to the original programme to support the Complex Communication Needs (CCN) of the participants. CCN is a term used to describe "those for whom gestural, speech and/or written communication is temporarily or permanently inadequate to meet all of their communication needs" (Beukelman & Miranda, 1998).

AIMS OF THE PROGRAMME

"Imagine, Create, Belong" has the overall aim of increasing a young person's social awareness. The programme does this through activities based on complex pretend play skills that involve representational thinking together with narrative ability and understanding of theory of mind. The specific aims of "Imagine, Create, Belong" are as follows.

1. To increase a young person's ability to logically sequence a narrative that involves more than two characters.

2. To increase a young person's ability to develop the story by introducing a "problem" into the narrative and resolve this problem through negotiation with one another.

3. To increase a young person's ability to talk through the narrative as they develop the story.

4. To increase a young person's ability to generate alternative answers to use of objects (related to object substitution ability in early pretend play and related to language and problem solving).

Longer-term outcomes

Two pilot studies of this programme demonstrated that there were measurable improvements in participants' flexible and sequential thinking, self-regulation, empathy, and awareness of self as a social being (Goldingay et al., 2015; Goldingay et al., under review). It is hypothesised that longer-term outcomes would relate to increased social awareness and increased ability to understand a social context through increased awareness of character development, related language development, and problem solving.

ADDITIONAL AIMS FOR ADOLESCENTS WHO ATTEND A SPECIAL SCHOOL

5. To increase participants' use of abstract and descriptive language concepts.

6. To increase participants' length of utterance and inclusion of pertinent information when constructing and recalling narrative.

7. To include and increase participants' use of Augmentative and Alternative Communication (AAC) strategies.

Longer-term outcomes for adolescents at special school

This programme has been run several times at a special developmental school in Victoria, Australia, and anecdotally observed outcomes have included: improvements in participants' flexible thinking, self-regulation, and empathy. It is hypothesised that longer-term outcomes would relate to increased social awareness and increased ability to understand a social context through increased awareness of character development, related language development, and problem solving.

In adolescence: Insight into understanding of social rules, social perceptiveness, perception of context – emotional and social, autobiographical narrative, stories and narrative, formulation of arguments

Complex pretend play in pre-adolescence underpinning ability in: Representational thought (object substitution (symbols in play), reference to absent objects, attribution of properties). Reference to something or someone outside of self (decentration), social pretend play, role play with emersion of characters in the play. Logical sequential thought in a narrative, flexibility and adaptability in thinking, emotion regulation, metacognition, 'metaplay' (talking about the play as you play)

Figure 2.1 Underpinning ability of pretend play for adolescence

ABOUT THE MANUAL

This facilitator manual is for teachers, therapists, or other health professionals who are running the programme. It is recommended that facilitators are familiar with working with adolescents who are neuro-diverse and have had 12 months or more experience in this area.

This manual is not prescriptive because the programme is person-centred in approach. The manual is a guide for how to run "Imagine, Create, Belong" on a session-by-session basis. Therefore, a range of activities will be suggested for each week and the facilitator can use their discretion as to which activity will suit their particular group in their current stage of development. This manual acts as a template with ideas and specific activities, but these can be adjusted up or down to match the young people's level. It helps to revise the following week's activities in light of how the group went the previous week.

The activities have been carefully designed and each activity is underpinned by a range of evidence-based theoretical frameworks relevant to social development work with neuro-diverse young people (see Chapter 1 for a background on the underpinning theoretical foundations of "Imagine, Create, Belong").

FACILITATORS

At least two facilitators are recommended to run "Imagine, Create, Belong" because it is a small group format. This allows for a greater level of observation and interaction with participants. Each group will have different dynamics. While one facilitator is running the activity the other can be observing and supporting where needed. The facilitator needs to be flexible, comfortable with uncertainty, and trusting of the process. The facilitator responds to the participants with congruence, unconditional positive regard, and empathic understanding. Congruence is genuineness or authenticity. The facilitator is consistent within themselves. Their emotions are consistent with their verbal and non-verbal communication. Their own problems are "left at the door" and during the sessions the facilitator is totally present for the group. It may be beneficial to the facilitators to allow for some personal reflection time after each session as a way of processing emotions as well as gaining a deeper understanding of how the session went in preparation for the next session. If the facilitator finds this difficult, it is recommended that the facilitator also source their own personal therapy. Unconditional positive regard is accepting and not judging the young person. The principles given in Chapter 1 (p. 13) reflect unconditional positive regard. Empathic understanding can be shown through empathic reflection where the facilitator acknowledges the young person's emotions within their involvement of the activities. For example, the facilitator may say, "Making your character was very frustrating, but you did it. Your character has hair, arms, and legs just like you discussed", "You seem overwhelmed. I wonder if you would like to just sit and think for a while. Here is a squeeze ball that you liked last session", "You are pleased with the final result". Making a point of observing and pointing out strengths and positive actions is also important, no matter how small. Neuro-diverse young people, while not a homogenous group, may have abilities and strengths not seen as often among neuro-typical groups the same age. Examples include but are not limited to: thinking about topics in original and fresh ways; thinking deeply about topics; being able to focus on and remember details about topics they are interested in; being helpful, kind, honest, and generous, and maintaining independent thought even when in a group.

When supporting participants with CCN, facilitators must be aware of strategies and tools used to support their receptive language understanding and allow them to use expressive language. This may involve the use of visual supports and AAC strategies. Consideration must be given to what words and functions of communication each participant may need to access in any given session and how they will do so. When working with participants with CCN, it is advised that you consult with their treating speech pathologist.

When conducting the programme in a special school setting where additional staff including teachers and education support staff are available to participate in the programme, it is important to provide education regarding key concepts within the programme. This may involve an informal after-school session each week and coaching during sessions.

THE ORGANISATION OF SESSIONS AND ACTIVITIES IN CHAPTERS 3–10

"Imagine, Create, Belong" is divided into eight sessions, but each session may be run over one or more sessions depending on the needs of the group you are facilitating. The latter is particularly relevant if you are working with adolescents with additional needs in a special school. Chapters 3–10 present the detail for the eight sessions of "Imagine, Create, Belong", with one chapter dedicated to one session. For example, Chapter 3 is Session 1, Chapter 4 is Session 2, and so on.

Each session is divided into Section A and Section B. Section A is for those in mainstream settings (for adolescents whose Intelligence Quota (IQ) score is greater than or equal to 70) and Section B is for adolescents with additional needs, for example those attending special education settings (for those with an IQ score of less than or equal to 70).

In each chapter, for each session, the chapter begins with what to expect and gives the aim of the session. Theories underpinning the session are listed with hints on how to set up the session to be consistent with the underlying principles of "Imagine, Create, Belong". A facilitators' toolkit is then given, listing what resources the facilitator needs to prepare for each session. This list is followed by an introduction to the session and the session outline. In this section, some hints may be given on how to enact the principles of the person-centred approach and create a zone of proximal development. The activities for the session are divided into four, which cover: the warm up activity; the tuning in activity; the active phase, which is the core activity of "Imagine, Create, Belong" – the development of a cohesive movie narrative; and a closure activity.

Each session's activities is organised into four parts, as noted in the paragraph above. These four parts are replicated for both Section A and Section B. That is, Section A has four parts and Section B has four parts. The four parts are: 1) a warm up activity; 2) a tuning in activity; 3) the active phase; 4) the closure phase. Given that some of this work involves participants' self and identity, it is important to enable the opportunity to close the session and debrief.

Each chapter is set out in the following order:

1. What should I expect – this gives the aim of the session

2. Theories underpinning the session – this relates to the aim of the session

3. Section A: For adolescents from mainstream schools

   Facilitators' toolkit – resources needed for this session

   Introduction and session outline – how to enact the principles of the person-centred approach and create a zone of proximal development

   Warm up activity

   Tuning in activity

   Action activity

   Closure activity

4. Section B: For adolescents attending special schools (suggestions given in Section B for this session to cover more than one session)

   Facilitators' toolkit – resources needed for this session

   Warm up activity – suggestions given over two sessions

   Tuning in activity – suggestions given over two sessions

   Action activity – suggestions given over two sessions

   Closure activity – suggestions given over two sessions

THE ACTIVITIES

The activities given throughout "Imagine, Create, Belong" reflect the aims of the programme which, in turn, are underpinned and supported by the theoretical approaches outlined in Chapter 1 (p. 7). None of the activities are isolated tasks as all activities work towards enabling the development of the young person's social skills.

In summary, the activities are based on the key skills involved in complex pretend play. These key skills are informed by Learn to Play Therapy (Stagnitti, 1998, 2016a, 2016b, 2017a, 2017b). They include the ability to: self-initiate a play idea and develop a cohesive play script; sequence play actions logically and sequentially; use object substitutions within the play scenario as well as absent objects and property attributions; use characters as if alive within the play (decentre from self); role play; embed problems in the play and resolve them; and engage in co-operative play with others. Using Vygotsky's (1934/1986) analogy of "geological layers", the following areas of ability are the "geological layers" of the concepts behind "Imagine, Create, Belong" and the play skills are spread across these layers. For example, theory of mind includes the play skills of decentring from self, role play, and socially co-operating, while development of narrative includes initiating an idea for a play script, logical, sequential actions, and decentring from self. To have socially meaningful interactions in the world, all these areas and skills need to be integrated, so there is "leaking" from one "geological layer" into another. For example, theory of mind "leaks" into "development of narrative" (Douglas & Stirling, 2016).

The areas or "layers" below summarise the concepts behind the skills, which are the focus of "Imagine, Create, Belong". The last three areas also incorporate the person-centred approach of the facilitator.

Building relationships

Relationships are key in a child's learning. Relationships that foster warmth and pleasure help a child to regulate their attention to allow new learning to take place. Children develop "learning relationships" that help them to progress in their development (Greenspan & Wieder, 2006, p. 40). Relationships contribute to a child's social-emotional system. Relationships create a feeling of safety that supports a child's growth (Booth & Jernberg, 2010). This is underpinned by Vygotsky's socio-cultural model, particularly the zone of proximal development, and person-centred therapy.

Theory of mind

Development of empathy in "Imagine, Create, Belong" is fostered through the creation of a character and giving it attributes, feelings, and thoughts which are different to the self. This reflects the pretend play skill of decentring from self (Stagnitti, 2016a). These activities require the participant to take the perspective of another, and to answer questions based on what the other person knows. The use of activities focused on theory of mind links into the final goal of creating the narrative and the movie.

Development of narrative

Development of narrative requires logical sequencing, cause and effect, and problem solving (Stagnitti, 2016a). The activities aimed at consolidating narrative thinking are not splinter skills but form part of the complexity of social interaction, as social interaction involves the understanding of context, building ideas from one to another, and autobiographical narrative understanding. These skills play a vital role in the retell of events and in the prediction of consequences for actions. Providing a retell involves perspective taking, consideration for the background knowledge of the listener (Stringer, 2006).

Representational thinking

Representational thinking occurs in pretend play and is the ability to go beyond the literal. Object substitution is the ability to use an object as a symbol for something else. For example, a box represents a car. Representational thinking can also include the attribution of properties to objects (for example, the character is angry) and reference to absent objects (for example, a storm). Representational thinking is higher level thinking.

The areas below incorporate the person-centred approach of the facilitator to provide a zone of proximal development and support to the young person during "Imagine, Create, Belong".

Sensory processing

Recognising individual differences in the way young people process sensory information enables the facilitators to support the young person to participate in a calm alert state. For example, young people who cannot sit in close proximity to others are offered alternative seating arrangements, such as sitting with the group on a chair (Dunn, 2007) or sitting away from the group in the first sessions until the young person feels more comfortable sitting closer. Recognising sensory individual differences is also consistent with person-centred therapy approaches.

Neuro-responsive social scaffolding

The facilitator responds to the young person's neuro-divergence by scaffolding social interactions alongside use of supportive objects or calming activities. Scaffolding of skills is done in a progressive way and is informed from constructivist ideas from the work of Vygotsky (1934/1986). When applied to scaffolding social skills in an eight-session programme for neuro-diverse young people, it means the expectations and sociability of the activities are gradually increased over the course of the programme. Young people are supported through the person-centred skills of the facilitators to engage at their own pace and with the use of props or supports of their choosing. These may include electronic devices, stress balls, or other items.

Linguistic competence

For young people who have developmental difficulties and attend special school, awareness of participants' individual linguistic abilities to scaffold their access to content enables the facilitator to respond at the level where the young person can understand and engage in the task. Consideration should be given to each participant's receptive understanding of language to inform how information must be presented. For example, reducing background noise and complexity of speech, and the use of Visually Supported Communication or Visually Mediated Communication (Hodgdon, 1995), for instance, the use of visual supports including pictures, gesture, and demonstration, are vital here. In the programme, participants' individual AAC systems assist participants to engage at a deeper level. Participants should have access to appropriate communication tools that enable access to a wide range of single words to meet a variety of communicative functions, including: expression of wants, needs and emotions; to request help and information; to reject and to comment on their world (Light, 1988). It is advised that facilitators consult with the participants' treating speech pathologist, classroom teacher, or parent to determine what communication tools they will require to access the programme. Be aware that for many participants Multimodal communication will be used. Multimodal communication involves a combination of "modes" to get a message across, such as verbal speech, speech generated from an electronic device, gesture, Auslan or Key Word Signs, picture symbols, or object symbols (holding or exchanging an object to convey a message). All intelligible messages should be acknowledged and responded to and support provided to interpret communication attempts following a communication breakdown.

PREPARATION FOR SESSION 1

Before your first group session (Session 1) for "Imagine, Create, Belong", make contact with the young people who will be attending. The form of the contact depends on your group. You may contact face to face, as you work with the young people in a school setting or community setting. Contact may be electronic, via email, a messaging app, text message, or whatever is appropriate or relevant for the young people you will be or are working with.

During this contact, thank the young person for their interest in coming to "Imagine, Create, Belong" and explain to them what will be involved. That is, they will join other young people, similar to themselves, imagine they are the writers, producers, and directors of a movie, and create a movie story together. Depending on the young people you work with, the reason for the group could be: because they feel socially isolated and would like to make some friends; because they find schooling difficult and would like to do something different for some of the school day; because they like movies; because they would like to learn how to socialise with peers; and so on.

When you meet the young person, ask them to bring an item from home with them that they would be willing to tell the other participants about. This is important for the first session as it lets the young person know that they are unique, that you are interested in what they find interesting, and it also provides an avenue for them to begin to think about their own autobiographical narrative. As facilitators, you need to remember to bring your own item from home that you are willing to talk about with the group as well, so you can set the tone for the first session, and participants can begin to relate to you as well. For all sessions it is most important for the participants to feel accepted, so avoid placing demands on them such as eye contact or speaking up in the group.

CONCLUSION

This chapter has outlined the aims of "Imagine, Create, Belong" for young people who are neuro-diverse and attend mainstream schools and special schools. How the manual is organised is explained, particularly for the remaining Chapters 3–10. The structure of how each session of "Imagine, Create, Belong" is provided, with further information underpinning the activities. The remaining chapters follow the same format as each chapter outlines the individual sessions for "Imagine, Create, Belong". The next chapter, Chapter 3, outlines Session 1 of "Imagine, Create, Belong".

REFERENCES

Beukelman, D., & Miranda, P. (1998). *Augmentative and alternative communication: Management of severe communication disorders in children and adults* (2nd ed.). Baltimore: Brooke's Publishing.

Booth, P. B., & Jernberg, A. M. (Eds) (2010). *Theraplay. Helping parents and children build better relationships through attachment-based play* (3rd ed.). San Francisco, CA: John Wiley & Sons.

Douglas, S., & Stirling, L. (2016). The intersection of pretense and storytelling in children with autism spectrum disorder. In S. Douglas & L. Stirling (Eds), *Children's play, pretense, and story: Studies in culture, context, and autism spectrum disorder* (pp. 117–146). New York: Psychology Press.

Dunn, W. (2007). Supporting children to participate successfully in everyday life by using sensory processing knowledge. *Infants & Young Children*, 20(2), 84–101.

Goldingay, S., Stagnitti, K., Robertson, N., Sheppard, L., Dean, B., & Pepin, G. (under review). Group comparison intervention to facilitate social skills in a group of adolescents.

Goldingay, S., Stagnitti, K., Sheppard, L., McGillivray, J., McLean, B., & Pepin, G. (2015). An intervention to improve social participation for adolescents with autism spectrum disorder: Pilot study. *Developmental Neurorehabilitation*, 18(2), 122–130.

Greenspan, S.I,. & Wieder, S. (2006). *Engaging autism.* Cambridge, MA: Da Capo Press.

Hodgdon, L. A. (1995). *Visual strategies for improving communication: Practical supports for school and home.* Michigan: QuirkRoberts Publishing.

Light, J. (1988). Interaction involving individuals using AAC systems: State of the art and future directions. *Augmentative and Alternative Communication*, 4(2), 66–82.

Stagnitti, K. (1998). *Learn to Play. A practical programme to develop imaginative play skills.* Melbourne: Co-ordinates Publishing.

Stagnitti, K. (2016a). Play, narrative, and children with autism. In S. Douglas & L. Stirling (Eds), *Children's play, pretense, and story: Studies in culture, context, and autism spectrum disorder* (pp. 51–71). New York: Psychology Press.

Stagnitti, K. (2016b). Play therapy for school-age children with high functioning autism. In A. Drewes & C. Schaefer (Eds), *Play therapy in middle childhood* (pp. 237–255). New York: American Psychological Association.

Stagnitti, K. (2017a). A growing brain – a growing imagination. In E. Prendiville & J. Howard (Eds), *Creative psychotherapy. Applying the principles of neurobiology to play and expressive arts-based practice* (pp. 183–200). London: Routledge.

Stagnitti, K. (2017b). *Parent Learn to Play facilitators manual.* Melbourne: Learn to Play.

Stringer, H. (2006). Facilitating narrative and social skills in secondary school students with language and behaviour difficulties. In J. Clegg & J. Ginsborg (Eds), *Language and social disadvantage. Theory into practice* (pp. 199–206). Chichester: John Wiley & Sons.

Vygotsky, L. (1934/1986). *Thought and language.* (Trans. and edited by Alex Kozulin). London: MIT Press.

CHAPTER 3

Session 1: Setting the scene

WHAT SHOULD I EXPECT?

This chapter outlines Session 1 for "Imagine, Create, Belong". Within this chapter, there are two main sections – Section A and Section B. Section A is for young people in their early to mid-adolescence who may be neuro-diverse and attend a mainstream school (Intelligence Quota (IQ) score is greater than or equal to 70). Section B is for young people who have additional needs and attend a special school (for those with an IQ score of less than or equal to 70). In Section B, Session 1 is expanded to cover two sessions across two weeks because young people with additional needs require more repetition.

These sections do not need to be adhered to rigidly and you may choose from Section A or Section B, depending on the needs, abilities, and interests of your group. With either group, prior to running your first session, ensure participants have been invited to bring to the group an item from home that they are willing to tell others about.

Session 1, this chapter, is organised in the following format. The aim of the session is outlined, then the underpinning theoretical models are listed with practical suggestions on how to approach the session (if applicable). Then Section A is presented. The facilitators' toolkit is provided, followed by how the facilitator introduces and outlines Session 1. The activities are made up of four parts, which are a warm up activity, a tuning in activity, the action activity, and finally the closure. The action activity is the "core" activity that runs through all the sessions and is the development and production of a movie. Given that some of this work involves participants' self and identity, it is important to enable the opportunity to close the session and debrief. Section A is followed by Section B. Section B has a similar format to Section A, except that activities are given for two sessions and the activities are geared for young people with special needs due to developmental difficulties.

The sessions can be carried out once a week, twice a week, or fortnightly. You choose the timing of the sessions to suit your group and circumstances.

AIMS OF SESSION 1

- Create a safe predictable group environment, form positive connections, set ground rules, boundaries, and culture of group, scaffolding participation for neuro-diverse teens.

- Plant the seed for participants to see themselves as the creators and storytellers (via an item from home and favourite movie).

- Plant the seeds for processes to keep participants on task, taking turns, and working together.

- Start developing modelling clay or woodblock character and characterisation (solitary activity).

Aims 1 and 3 are to create a safe, predictable group environment and to form positive connections between facilitators and participants, and between participants themselves. To provide a safe and predictable group setting, the ground rules, boundaries, and the "culture" of the group is set out. For adolescents who are neuro-diverse, scaffolding participation, accepting them unconditionally, and creating a socially safe environment may include enabling group members to have their electronic devices or other "comfort" items with them so that they feel safe to participate, and feel understood and accepted by facilitators.

The second aim of this first session is to orientate participants to seeing themselves as the creators of story and narrative (initiating an idea of a story), including having the opportunity to voice their own narrative about what is important to them when talking about their object from home. This is preparing them for the following sessions where they will explore their own identity in more detail with the use of a genogram and ecomap or Tree of Life.[1] Following on from this, the young people begin to consider the identity of the character they will be creating. Please remember that if you are working from Section B, you will run Session 1 over two sessions.

THEORIES, ABILITIES, AND APPROACHES UNDERPINNING SESSION 1

- Person-centred therapy.

- Development of narrative through age-appropriate pretend play skills.

- Neuro-responsive social scaffolding, which is a concept that builds on the social constructivist model of Vygotsky and Rogers and relates to the social challenges faced by neuro-diverse people (see Chapter 1).

Suggestions for approaching this session

This first session, Session 1, is when everyone is finding their place in where they might belong in the group. Your skills as a facilitator are critical in setting up a safe, predictable environment where the young person feels warmly welcomed and accepted for who they are. You can reflect the unconditional acceptance of your participants by explaining that in each session the format will be similar, and you might like to say a little about who you are and you can do this gently by bringing something to the group that you feel comfortable talking about. In this session, you begin the process of gathering ideas for a movie. In this session, it is more likely that there will be lots of ideas and no overall, clear narrative play. This is to be expected; accept all ideas. During this session, the young people (participants) will be working together sometimes and then on their own at other times. Try not to ask too many questions of the group, and avoid singling out any participants in any activity. Even though talking about the object brought from home is individual, the whole group is participating. If, for your group, there is a young person who didn't bring something, do not make any fuss about this, and offer the young person an alternative, such as inviting them to mention any interests they may have.

If you are working in a community-based service and the group has been specifically designed and run, and so the participants would not normally see each other during the week, then it is important to prepare for closure at the start of working together. One way to prepare them is by weekly prompts towards the end of the programme (for example, Session 6) regarding how many sessions to go.

SECTION A: SUGGESTIONS FOR MAINSTREAM SCHOOL SETTINGS

Reminder: When planning this session, remember to ensure participants have been invited to bring to the group an item from home that they are willing to tell others about.

FACILITATORS' TOOLKIT

Balloons – a face is drawn on one of the balloons and the balloon is inflated

Strength cards (see Appendix 2 – have in reserve in case needed)

Whiteboard marker

Toy (for example, monkey)

Blank storyboard sheets (see Appendix 1)

Oven hardening or air drying modelling clay

INTRODUCTIONS AND SESSION OUTLINE (10 MINUTES)

1. Welcome to all participants. Introductions. Facilitators introduces themselves. Then invite the young people to go around the group and introduce themselves by saying their name.

2. As the facilitator, you introduce to the group what will be happening throughout the programme and the structure of each session.

3. Ethos of programme. As a facilitator working within a person-centred approach, you work with the participants at the stage they are at and make no judgements (see person-centred principles in Chapter 1 (p. 13) as well as the section on p. 41).

4. In this introduction, also give an orientation to the space the group is working in – for example, where the toilets are, use of electronic devices is welcome and can be used throughout sessions, etc. Outline here the rules of the group such as: respect the person who is talking by listening to what they are saying. Ask the young people if they would like any other rules. Add anything further here that is relevant to the group you are working with.

5. Let the group know what they can do if anyone needs a break, for example, giving an option for a safe space to retreat to if anyone is feeling overwhelmed. For young people who are neuro-diverse, be aware that they can become overwhelmed and that their memory for what was planned from one session to another may not be strong. As a facilitator, keep your own notes of ideas and suggestions that the group comes up with or use butchers' paper; if appropriate, ask a young person to be a scribe of ideas on the butchers' paper. "Imagine, Create, Belong" is for young people who are neuro-diverse, so, as a facilitator, be prepared for ideas to ebb and flow from session to session.

WARM UP ACTIVITY (10 MINUTES)

There are three activities for this first warm up. As a facilitator, you may find you cover all three with your group, or you may find you only use one or two. How many warm up activities you get through depends on your group. If you do not use some of these in this session, you may want to use some in other sessions.

1. This is an activity for the whole group. As a facilitator, take an inflated balloon and draw a face on it (alternatively, you may have

also drawn a face on it before the session). With the group, decide on a name for the face. Tell the group that we are going to try to keep the balloon in the air. The facilitator throws the balloon up in the air and, together with the group, keeps it in the air for as long as possible. If the group would like to repeat this activity, ask if there is anyone who would like to throw the balloon. If there is no volunteer, then the facilitator throws the balloon and invites the group to help keep the balloon in the air. The second facilitator times how long the balloon stays in the air.

2. Go around the group again, with each person saying their name to remind the group of everyone's name. The facilitator then asks participants to say their name with an adjective before it that they have thought up, for example, Super Sammy, Clever Sammy, Boisterous Ben. This is practice in property attributions because the adjective added is not physically visible and is an imposed meaning by the young person. For the first session, the facilitator may begin.

3. As this next activity requires an increase in memory capacity, be sensitive to the group as a facilitator and make a decision whether including this next activity would overwhelm the group and be too tiring to include in this first session or whether the group would enjoy it. If you decide it would be too taxing on the group, then proceed to the tuning in activity. If you decide this third activity would be fun, then this activity requires a toy (for example, a monkey). The facilitator gets the toy and throws it to another person in the group, saying the person's name with the adjective before you throw it. That is, "Catch the monkey, Clever Sammy". The person in the group (in this instance, "Clever Sammy") who catches the toy, throws it to another person, saying the person's name with the adjective.

TUNING IN ACTIVITY (10 MINUTES)

You can choose to split your group into pairs or threes or keep the entire group together for this activity, depending on the size of your group and the preferences and abilities of your participants. Invite participants to speak about the thing that they have chosen to bring in with them.

Give each person a 2–5 minute time limit to speak about their favourite thing. Let the group know that they have a time limit and everyone has the same time limit. Have the second facilitator do the timing. Depending on the group, the facilitator may start. Otherwise, nominate where to begin in the group (for example, one end, the middle).

If the young person gets stuck, provide a prompt such as the following:

- I was wondering why you chose to bring in that item?
- I was wondering if it is your favourite thing?
- How long have you had it?
- How much time do you spend playing with it?

ACTION ACTIVITY (15 MINUTES)

Introduction to directing your own movie

The facilitator explains that in this programme we are going to be movie producers and we will be making a script for a movie that we will record at the end of the programme. In this action activity, there are sections where the participants will work on their own and there are sections where they will come together as a group. As the programme is aimed for early to mid-adolescents who are neuro-diverse, it is important as a facilitator that you respond to the group and shift the activity from group to solitary and back as needed.

Explain to the participants that they will be creating the story together: they are all the directors or script writers. The facilitator then invites participants to get into pairs and share with each other what their favourite movie is and why. Is it the characters? The theme? The special effects? The music? What sort of movie would they like to create?

When the facilitator observes that the group is ready to move to the next stage of the activity, invite the participants to come together as a group and pool their ideas for what sort of movie each pair would like to create. Use the blank storyboard sheets (see Appendix 1) and hand them around the group, or alternatively, use one blank storyboard sheet and start to pool ideas onto the one sheet. At this stage of

"Imagine, Create, Belong", there are more likely to be divergent ideas of the narrative (that is, plot) of the movie. In this session, pooling the ideas gives the group awareness of the range of movie ideas. It also shows that you, as facilitator, respect all the ideas put forward. As a facilitator, this session may feel chaotic as all the participants will most probably have divergent ideas on what movie they would like to create. This is to be expected and, in the first session, the facilitator accepts all ideas and records them.

After this discussion, the facilitator then moves the activity to a solitary phase. The facilitator brings in the modelling clay and starts to play with it. When the facilitator has the group's attention, the facilitator invites participants to consider what they would like their movie character to be: a hero, a victim, a villain, a guide, a love interest, boy/girl next door, etc. The facilitator then hands out the modelling clay and invites participants to make their own characters out of it. Have a range of colours available to allow maximum opportunities for the group in the creation of their character. Allow participants to use alternative materials if they prefer, for example, adhesive putty.

CLOSURE ACTIVITY (5 MINUTES)

Ask participants to say what they enjoyed most. Remind participants of the next session and the activities they will do. Pack up and finish.

SECTION B: FOR ADOLESCENTS WITH ADDITIONAL NEEDS

Please note the content of Session 1 is delivered over two sessions for Section B. For convenience, the breakdown of Session 1 into two sessions will be referred to as: Session 1 Week 1 and Session 1 Week 2.

FACILITATORS' TOOLKIT

Visual schedule (see Appendix 3)

Bean-filled toy (can be any weighted soft toy)

Strength cards (see Appendix 2 for explanation. Can be sourced commercially or made up in the group)

Participant's favourite item

Blank storyboard sheets (see Appendix 1)

A short video clip, for example, Pixar's *Knick Knack* https://YouTu.be/9uhM_SUhdaw

Visual supports, including commonalities cards (to be created by facilitator – see Appendix 4) for closure activity

A large red dot, a large blue dot

Note to facilitators: Session 1 is an introduction to making a movie and the storyboard because this takes many sessions to master. The activities in Session 1 Week 2 are required in preparation for the genogram and ecomap or Tree of Life, which will be introduced in Session 2. The activities in Session 1 Week 2 explicitly teach how to identify the physical characteristics of a character. This is important to establish before introducing the genogram in Session 2. These concepts might be challenging for participants undertaking Section B. More information is given in Session 2 on genograms (see Chapter 4).

INTRODUCTION

Session 1 Week 1 and Week 2

The facilitator welcomes the young people (participants) to the group and directs the participants' attention to a group visual schedule, which will include an outline of the programme. If required, provide orientation to the environment (for example, where the toilets are). Depending on the group, the facilitator may also have a safe space set up (for example, a quiet area with minimal visual stimulation) for those participants who may need a break during the session, for instance, for those who get overwhelmed. See Appendix 3 for information on how to use a visual schedule.

WARM UP ACTIVITY

Session 1 Week 1: Throwing bean-filled toy

Invite the whole group to sit in a circle (this can be on the floor or on a chair). The facilitator models how to orient your body towards another young person, gain their attention by speaking or waving (or whatever would be appropriate), and greet them. This may be done verbally, gesturally or through an individual's Augmentative or Alternative Communication (AAC) system. When the facilitator has observed that all members know how to do this, then the facilitator throws the bean-filled toy to a group member. The facilitator reflects any prosocial behaviour observed, for example, "I noticed you facing John".

Session 1 Week 2: Strength card introductions

Invite the whole group to sit in a circle (this can be on the floor or on a chair). The facilitator spreads out the strength cards, face up, on the floor or table in the middle of the group. The facilitator then invites the young people to select a strength card from the middle of the circle. Each participant is then given the opportunity to introduce themselves with their name and the strength they have chosen – for example "I'm Sally and I'm strong". As an option to the young person verbally expressing themselves, the facilitator can suggest participants express their strength with their body (facial expression or body movement). The facilitator demonstrates this.

Note: These activities are repeated in the final week of the programme. You may wish to film in Session 1 Week 1 for evaluation purposes, but seek appropriate written consents from parents/guardians with an outline of where this film will be shown and for what purpose.

TUNING IN ACTIVITY

Session 1 Week 1

For Session 1 Week 1, the young person has brought in an item from home that they are comfortable presenting to the group. Depending on the size of your group and their confidence, split the group into two or place the young people in pairs. The young person speaks about the item that they have chosen to bring in with them from home. Give each person a 2-minute time limit to speak about their favourite item. The timer can be a visual timer or the facilitator may indicate by their hand when 1 minute is up and then 2 minutes is up. Provide the following prompts if needed:

- I was wondering why you chose to bring in that item?
- Is it your favourite thing?
- How long have you had it?
- How much time do you spend playing with it? Etc.

Session 1 Week 2

- For this whole-group activity, invite everyone to sit on the floor in a circle. Each member of the group has a box *or* drum (half the group with boxes and half with drums).

- The facilitator says "Everyone with a drum, start playing; everybody with a box, listening only". After 20 seconds of playing, the leader calls for "stop".

- Repeat the activity with boxes: "Everyone with a box start playing; everybody with a drum, listening only". After 20 seconds of playing, the leader calls for "stop".

- The facilitator begins discussion around the differences in the sound, look, and feel of boxes and drums (see Appendix 4, Table A4.1, for a chat board example). It may be helpful to construct a "chat board" with key vocabulary required for this activity.

ACTION ACTIVITY

Session 1 Week 1

The action activity is an introduction to directing your own movie.

- The facilitator invites the group to watch a short (up to 5 minutes) video through once, uninterrupted. This video requires a minimum of two characters and a well-defined goal, problem, and solution. The facilitator may select a short clip from a movie that participants know and like, or an unfamiliar short film such as Pixar's *Knick Knack* that meets this criteria.

- The facilitator models story development and storyboard (see Appendix 1) based on the engaging short clip (for example, Pixar's *Knick Knack*).

- Watch video through once again uninterrupted.

- The group rewatches the video and the facilitator pauses the video to encourage discussion on the story in the video. The aspects of the story that are highlighted by the facilitator are the characters, the characters' goal, the problem and solution, and the conclusion to the story. The facilitator prompts are by means of the following.

    - Characters 1 + 2 from the video clip: the facilitator supports the group to identify the main characters, for example, Snowman and the Miami girl.

    - Goal: the facilitator prompts with "What did the snowman want to do?"

    - Problem: the facilitator prompts with "Why couldn't he get to the girl?"

    - Solution: the facilitator prompts with "What did the snowman try to do to escape and be with the girl?"

    - Conclusion: the facilitator prompts with "What happened at the end? Did it work?"

- The facilitator explains to the group that they will each be writing a script for a movie that they will record at the end of the programme; however, for today the group will be working together to make one story. The facilitator chooses a participant to draw each element of the story onto a group storyboard, as the group brainstorms ideas supported by the facilitator.

    - Characters 1 + 2: the facilitator directs discussion for the group to choose characters that are familiar to the participants, for example, a teacher. Then the facilitator leads brainstorming of the characters' physical and personality characteristics.

- Goal: the goal of the story is introduced by the facilitator with a comment such as: "What is something they really want to do/have?" (prompts such as: to get to basketball with their students on time).

- Problem: the story has a problem and the facilitator prompts with a comment such as: "What is something that stops them from achieving their goal?" (prompts such as: the bus breaks down).

- Solution: the problem in the story needs a solution and the facilitator prompts with a comment such as: "How do they try to overcome their problem?" (prompts such as: call someone to help.)

Session 1 Week 2

The action activity for this session is to highlight the physical characteristics of the character in the story. The story from the previous session is maintained.

Introduction to physical characteristics (hair, height, eye colour, boy/girl).

- The facilitator models this activity first with a familiar staff member. The facilitator discusses with the group the characteristics of that staff member and completes the worksheet with information from the group. (For the worksheet see visual supports in Appendix 4.)

- The facilitator then invites the group to move to tables to begin the small group activity (one staff member to two–three participants). With support from staff members, the young people complete the same worksheet about themselves.

- Movement activity: the facilitator introduces a game and asks a young person from the group to help with the game. The young person places a red dot in the room and a blue dot in a different

Table 3.1 Tally board

Hair	Hair colour	Eye colour	Height	Boy	Girl
Curly	Blonde				
Straight	Red				
Long	Black				
Short	Brown				

part of the room. The game is about physical characteristics of people in the group. The facilitator gives directions such as "If you have brown hair go to the red dot", "if you have curly hair go to the blue dot".

- Consolidation of physical characteristics: the facilitator constructs a tally board (this can be hard copy or interactive whiteboard; see Table 3.1) as per the table below. It is advised that picture supports be included in this, such as those available from Boardmaker™ or SymbolStix™. The tally board summarises the physical characteristic of the whole group.

- The facilitator reviews the tally board and comments on how some people look the same and some look different, just like we like some of the same things and others like different things.

CLOSURE ACTIVITY

Session 1 Week 1 and Week 2

Commonalities game

Prior to this session, the facilitator needs to make cards with guidance from prompts in Appendix 4. This game is repeated each session with a variation of focus. Having a similar game end every session provides a consistent routine for young people with additional needs. For Session 1 Weeks 1 and 2, the focus is on physical characteristics.

The group sits on chairs in a circle. However, the facilitator has organised the chairs so there is one less chair than there are participants. The facilitator begins by standing in the middle of the circle and choosing a prompt card made in preparation for the session (see Appendix 4). The facilitator reads from the visual prompt card, for example, "Stand up if you are wearing shoes". Once all the people wearing shoes are standing, the facilitator directs "Change places, go!" Individuals standing must find another chair in the circle to sit on before the facilitator sits. Whoever is left without a chair becomes the new leader. They have a choice between using a visual prompt from the bag or thinking of their own criteria. The game continues until the session time is up or all prompts have been used.

To finish the session, ask participants to share what they enjoyed the most. A visual choice board (for instruction on using a visual choice board, see https://youtu.be/fDN6_UUfIHQ; for symbols from the visual schedule, see Appendix 3) may be required to support participants to reflect on the session. The facilitator reminds participants of the next session and the activities they will do. The group packs up to finish.

NOTE

1 Tree of Life is a way of representing the self, family, and ancestry by drawing on the concepts of nature. The version presented in this manual was created by Wadawurrung Traditional Custodian Corrina Eccles (see Appendix 5).

CHAPTER 4

Session 2: Participants' life story and the life story of the character

WHAT SHOULD I EXPECT?

Welcome to Session 2. This chapter outlines Session 2 for "Imagine, Create, Belong". Within this chapter, there are two main sections – Section A and Section B. Section A is for young people in their early to mid-adolescence who may be neuro-diverse and attend a mainstream school (Intelligence Quota (IQ) score is greater than or equal to 70). Section B is for young people who have additional needs and attend a special school (for those with an IQ score of less than or equal to 70). In Section B, Session 2 is expanded to cover two sessions across two weeks because young people with additional needs require more repetition.

As in the previous session, these sections do not need to be adhered to rigidly and you may choose from Section A or Section B or a combination of both, depending on the needs, abilities, and interests of your group. You may also run Session 2 over one or more weeks depending on the needs, abilities, and interests of your group. The sessions can be carried out once a week, twice a week, or fortnightly. You choose the timing of the sessions to suit your group and circumstances.

Session 2, this chapter, is organised in the following format. The aims of the session are outlined, then the underpinning theoretical approaches and abilities are listed with practical suggestions on how to approach the session (if applicable). In this session, the facilitator is introducing an autobiographical activity and as this activity may raise some issues for the participant in the group, the facilitator needs to create a safe environment where the young people feel supported.

Then Section A is presented, with the facilitators' toolkit provided, followed by how the facilitator welcomes and outlines Session 2. The activities are in the following format: warm up activity; a tuning in activity; the action activity; and then the closure activity. Section A is followed by Section B. Given that some of this work in Session 2 involves participants' self and identity, it is important to enable the opportunity to close the session and debrief.

AIMS OF SESSION 2

- Develop skills in working together, taking turns, listening to others, and staying on task to continue group bonding and setting within a person-centred approach.

- Continue working on character with modelling clay (solitary activity).

- Begin process of character life story development (solitary activity) via genograms or Tree of Life (Appendix 5). This will help develop empathy and is a biographical narrative of the character. This session also includes an autobiographical narrative of the participant. Flexible thinking and problem solving are encouraged via object substitution.

THEORIES, ABILITIES, AND APPROACHES UNDERPINNING SESSION 2

- Person-centred approach.

- Representational thinking through symbolic play (using an object and pretending it is something else).

- Neuro-responsive social scaffolding.

- Theory of mind.

- Social constructivism (using stories from movies or books that are already well known to participants and building on this to develop theory of mind) (see Chapter 1).

Suggestions for approaching this session

This second session, Session 2, builds on the atmosphere that you, as a facilitator, created in Session 1. You may want to recap some of the introductory ground you covered to re-engage your participants. Your skills as a facilitator are critical in setting up a safe, predictable environment where the young person feels warmly welcomed and accepted of who they are. In this session, the participants should be less anxious; however, they will still need predictability in format so that their trust of the facilitators builds on Session 1. You can reflect the unconditional acceptance of your participants and build trust by explaining that in each session the format will be similar, by not asking too many questions of the group, and by ensuring that all participants are engaged in the same activities, if appropriate. As this session includes the autobiographical activity of creating a genogram and ecomap or Tree of Life, the facilitator needs to hold the group in a safe atmosphere. To do this, you may need to use empathic reflections such as: "You were brave to talk to us about that", "I can see that meant a lot to you", or "I wonder if you would like a break? That part of your story has a lot of feelings".

SECTION A: FOR MAINSTREAM SCHOOL SETTINGS

FACILITATORS' TOOLKIT

Paper plate

Miniature figurines for the theory of mind activity, with the story prepared beforehand

Butchers' paper

Felt-tip writing pens & adhesive putty

Blank A4 pieces of paper

Oven hardening or air drying modelling clay

Puppets

Piece of cloth (suggested size of a tea-towel)

INTRODUCTION

The facilitators welcome the group and provide a verbal outline of the session for the group. One facilitator may give a summary of some of the ideas the group has had about the movie.

WARM UP ACTIVITY (5–10 MINUTES)

Symbolic materials game

This activity assists participants to develop flexible thinking. A facilitator pulls out a piece of cloth or paper plate from the facilitators' toolkit. The facilitator invites the group to brainstorm and demonstrate alternate uses for the cloth, until no one can think of any more. Provide time for each participant to respond. Participants may act out their response and the facilitator can narrate and describe their actions. Write or draw the alternate uses on butchers' paper or a whiteboard. Keep the butchers' paper in a secure place for later.

Ideas for alternative uses of objects can be found in a free download of a book called *Pretending with objects* (Stagnitti, 2016), on the website learntoplayevents.com. Please note that the book is approximately 125 pages if you wish to print it.

TUNING IN ACTIVITY (10 MINUTES)

Theory of mind

Like all theory of mind tasks, this activity requires the participants to take the perspective of another, and to answer questions based on what the other person knows. Spend time talking with your group about movies, stories, or games they enjoy or know about. Examples could include Harry Potter books or movies, *Star Wars*®, Lego® movies, Mario Cart, Guardians of the Galaxy, Minecraft®, Roblox, etc. This discussion is important to build the group's engagement in the task to listen to others in the group who may have a different preference in movies to themselves.

After the discussion, devise a story using characters in a theory of mind story. As a facilitator, you will need to have prepared the stories before the group. For example, a theory of mind task can include a story of false belief (Hughes & Leekam, 2004). A false-belief story goes something like this:

> Mary puts her book on the shelf in the lounge room. Mary goes to her sister's room to see what she is doing. While she is away, her mother comes and takes the book and puts it in Mary's bedroom. Mary finishes talking to her sister and then goes to get her book. Where would she look for her book?

In this story, Mary has a false belief about where her book is. She thinks it is in the lounge room where she left it, but the reader knows that Mary has a false belief about where her book is, because the reader knows Mary's mother moved the book.

For Session 2, the theory of mind of false belief needs to be simple. That is, Person 1 has an object and puts it somewhere. Person 1 leaves, Person 2 sees the object and moves it. Person 1 comes back to get their object. Where does Person 1 look for their object?

Facilitators can use the story above or make up their own story using the components given above. For this activity, you, as the facilitator, tell the story as you move the figurines to act it out. This gives participants a visual picture of the story as well as the verbal telling of the story. As you tell the story, ask the group questions such as: "Where do you think [the character] will look for his/her [object]?" "Why do you think [the character] looked/went to [the space/place]?" Please also see the links below for example videos, which may be shown for an alternate learning method. The links are:

Sally, Ann, and the rabbit – where does Sally think the rabbit is?

www.youtube.com/embed/8nxJgsonjYw

Bailey, Sam, Liam – where does Sam think the boys are skating?

www.youtube.com/embed/VM2iefh0fJA

ACTION ACTIVITY (30 MINUTES)
Character development

This next activity begins the process of developing empathy, problem solving, and consequential thinking skills.

Part 1

The facilitator introduces the concept of a genogram and ecomap or Tree of Life[1] activity for participants. Genograms, ecomaps, and Tree of Life are explained with examples in Appendix 5. As the facilitator, model to the group your own genogram and ecomap of your parents, grandparents, life activities, and Tree of Life, and include people and pets. To ensure cultural safety for participants who may be Aboriginal or Torres Strait Islander, avoid crossing out deceased family members, even your own. Invite participants to choose which method they prefer for representing their family. Be alert to any signs of distress due to loss or grief issues for participants so you can follow up with the participant after the session to ensure they feel safe. As a facilitator, you may potentially engage school counselling services if needed. Depending on the group, invite them to explain their genogram and ecomap or Tree of Life in pairs or threes, or across the whole group. You may also decide not to discuss the genogram and ecomap or Tree of Life within the group.

Part 2

As a facilitator, you now invite participants to develop a genogram/ecomap or Tree of Life for the character they developed with the modelling clay in the previous session. Some participants may still need to do more work on the modelling clay character.

Part 3

When the participants have finished Part 2, invite each participant to think of a problem their character must solve and what their role might be. For example, are they a sidekick? A guide? A hero on a journey? A villain? A mad scientist? A rule breaker? Then, invite them to share the story of who their character is in pairs. Allow some time for the participants to share their story. While the participants are still in pairs, the facilitator extends the conversation between pairs by providing some ideas to the group about how their characters might interact with each other to solve their respective problems. For example, "Does the hero need to save someone and the mad scientist needs to test their invention?" "Does the hero need to find something or someone and the guide needs a protégé?"

Part 4

The facilitator then invites the pairs to come back to the whole group. Using butchers' paper or a whiteboard, the facilitator plots the beginnings of each storyline of each pair's character together with that pair. That is, the character is used by the facilitator to create the beginning of a storyline for each pair. This is preparation for Session 3, where there will be more development of the storyboard. As a facilitator, store this butchers' paper in a safe place to be used in Session 3. As a facilitator you accept the young people as they present each session. As young people who are neuro-diverse often have difficulty with memory, use the butchers' paper as a prompt to ideas that have been thought of. Throughout the sessions of "Imagine, Create, Belong", there will be many ideas about the movie that come and go. As a facilitator, you capture the main threads and bring these together with the group.

Part 5

Bringing it together. As a facilitator, remind the group of the ideas generated from the activity about alternative uses for the cloth. Then discuss with the group how the ideas generated from alternate uses of the cloth activity could be used for one or more storylines generated by the pairs in the group. Make a note of these ideas on another piece of butchers' paper. These ideas are the beginning of the group thinking about props and scenes for the movie.

CLOSURE ACTIVITY (5 MINUTES)

Invite the participants to say which of the session's activities they enjoyed the most and which they found the most challenging. If some young people in the group found some of the activities too challenging (for example, the genogram and ecomap, Tree of Life), then offer an alternative activity by inviting the participants to draw how they felt about the session or circle a visual representation of which activity was best for them, or rate the activities from 1 to 4. Make a note of their responses to build on for subsequent sessions. Pack up and finish. Say your goodbyes.

SECTION B: FOR ADOLESCENTS WITH ADDITIONAL NEEDS

Please note the content of Session 2 is delivered over two sessions for Section B. For convenience, the breakdown of Session 2 into two sessions will be referred to as: Session 2 Week 1 and Session 2 Week 2.

FACILITATORS' TOOLKIT

Visual schedule (see Appendix 3)

Storyboard

Cloth

Paper plate

Laminated cards containing favourite characters cut in half (postcards)

Beanbag (or weighted toy)

Visual supports for genogram (as required)

- Miniatures
- Photographs of participants and family members
- Line drawings of family members

Choice cards for commonalities. See appendix 6.

Picture cards with suggestions of activities, items or events the participants will like or dislike

INTRODUCTION

Session 2 Week 1 and Week 2

Facilitators welcome the participants to the group and direct participants' attention to a group visual schedule (refer to Appendix 3) which includes an outline of the session.

WARM UP ACTIVITY

Session 2 Week 1 and Week 2

Symbolic materials game

This activity assists participants to develop flexible thinking. A facilitator pulls out a piece of cloth (for Session 2 Week 1) or paper plate (For Session 2 Week 2) from the facilitators' toolkit. The facilitator invites the group to brainstorm and demonstrate alternate uses for the cloth, until no one can think of any more. Provide time for each participant to respond. Participants may act out their response and the facilitator can narrate and describe their actions. Write or draw the alternate uses on butchers' paper or a whiteboard. Keep the butchers' paper in a secure place for later.

Ideas for alternative uses of objects can be found in a free download of a book called *Pretending with objects* (Stagnitti, 2016) on the website learntoplayevents.com. Please note that the book is approximately 125 pages if you wish to print it.

TUNING IN ACTIVITY

Session 2 Week 1

Postcards

- The facilitators have prepared laminated cards with pictures of well-known characters on them, then cut the cards in half and placed the cut cards in a bag. Each card has half a picture of a well-known character. A facilitator invites the participants to choose a card from the bag. When all the participants have taken a card from the bag, the facilitator instructs the participants to locate their partner for the activity by finding the participant with the other half of the picture.

- When the participants have located their partner and pieced the two cards together, the pairs of participants work with a staff member to describe the physical characteristics and personality traits of their character (see Appendix 2 and/or 6 if the facilitators prefer the support of strength cards and choice cards for each physical characteristic). For example, Shrek is green, tall, smelly, grumpy, brave.

- When the pairs of participants have identified the physical characteristics of their character, the group reforms as a whole and each pair presents their findings to the group.

Session 2 Week 2
Beanbag greetings

- As a facilitator, invite the group to sit in a circle (on the floor or chairs depending on the needs of the group).

- Starting with a facilitator, each individual gains the attention of another person (for example, by saying someone's name or waving at someone). Once the attention of the participant is focused, the individual throws a beanbag towards the participant. The participant with the beanbag then attracts the attention of another participant and throws their beanbag. As a facilitator, ensure that a new person is chosen each time, so every member of the group has a turn.

- Once everyone has had a turn, repeat this activity with variation, that is, the person throwing the beanbag makes a face or pokes their tongue out and the person receiving the beanbag copies.

- Continue this until each participant has had two to three turns.

ACTION ACTIVITY

Session 2 Week 1

Genogram

- This activity utilises a genogram and ecomap or Tree of Life[2] activity for participants. Please see Appendix 5 for an explanation of a genogram and ecomap or Tree of Life. As the facilitator, model to the group your own genogram and ecomap of your parents, grandparents, life activities, and Tree of Life, and include people and pets. To ensure cultural safety for participants who may be Aboriginal or Torres Strait Islander, avoid crossing out deceased family members, even your own. Invite participants to choose which method they prefer for representing their family. Be alert to any signs of distress due to loss or grief issues for participants to follow up with the participant after the session and potentially engage school counselling services if needed.

- Provide visual supports such as photos of participants and their family or generic pictures of family members including pets. You may also like to provide line drawings of a family group or create a family grouping with miniatures that the participant chooses to represent individuals in their genogram.

Session 2 Week 2

Creating Character 1

- A facilitator models manipulation of a puppet. They then introduce the puppet as Character 1, independent from themselves. For example, the puppet may talk in a different voice and like eating things the facilitator doesn't like.

- The facilitator invites each participant to choose a puppet. Participants work in pairs with a facilitator or staff member to explore the puppet and think about its characteristics, including naming the puppet.

- As the participants work in pairs, each participant now draws their character on their own storyboard and writes down the characteristics of the character. (Note that this will be used for their story).

- The facilitator now divides the group into two groups. The size of the groups may vary based on individual participant abilities, for example, minimally verbal participants and those who utilise Augmentative and Alternative Communication (AAC) systems may require more time to share. Participants take turns to introduce their character to their group by manipulating the puppet, including voice and body posture. It may be useful to film this to review participants' ability to present their ideas.

CLOSURE ACTIVITY

Session 2 Week 1 and Week 2

Commonalities game

For this closure activity, the focus of questions is preferences, likes, and dislikes. Versions of this activity are used as the closure activity after each session. This builds a sense of security and predictability for the participants.

A facilitator organises participants to sit on chairs in a circle, and ensures there is one less chair than there are participants. The facilitator begins by standing in the middle of the circle and choosing a prompt card from a selection of prompt cards held in their hand. The facilitator reads from the visual prompt card, for example, "Stand up if you like cake". The facilitator draws awareness to the differences between participants' interests and preferences. Once all the people who like cake are standing, the facilitator directs "Change places, go!" Individuals standing must find another chair in the circle to sit on before the facilitator sits. Whoever is left without a chair becomes the new leader. They have a choice between using a visual prompt from the bag or thinking of their own criteria. The game continues until the session time is up or all prompts have been used.

The facilitator then asks participants to share what they enjoyed most. A visual choice board (for instruction on using a visual choice board, see https://youtu.be/fDN6_UUfIHQ; for symbols from the visual schedule – see Appendix 3) may be required to support participants to reflect on the session. Remind participants of the next session and the activities they will do. Pack up and finish.

NOTES

1 The Tree of Life presented in this manual was developed by Wadawurrung Traditional Custodian Corrina Eccles. It is a culturally appropriate tool to use with Aboriginal or Torres Strait Islander participants, but all participants should be invited to choose to use it.
2 The Tree of Life presented in this manual was developed by Wadawurrung Traditional Custodian Corrina Eccles. It is a culturally appropriate tool to use with Aboriginal or Torres Strait Islander participants, but all participants should be invited to choose to use it.

REFERENCES

Stagnitti, K. (2016). *Pretending with objects*. Retrieved from www.learntoplayevents.com/product/pretending-with-objects/

Hughes, C., & Leekam, S. (2004). What are the links between theory of mind and social relations? Review, reflections, and new directions for studies of typical and atypical development. *Social Development, 13*, 590–619. doi:10.1111/j.1467-9507.2004.00285.x

CHAPTER 5

Session 3: Narrative and identity: How does your character act and feel?

WHAT SHOULD I EXPECT?

Welcome to Session 3. This chapter outlines Session 3 for "Imagine, Create, Belong". Within this chapter, there are two main sections – Section A and Section B. Section A is for young people in their early to mid-adolescence who may be neuro-diverse and attend a mainstream school (Intelligence Quota (IQ) score is greater than or equal to 70). Section B is for young people who have additional needs and attend a special school (for those with an IQ score of less than or equal to 70). In Section B, Session 3 is expanded to cover two sessions across two weeks because young people with additional needs require more repetition.

As in the previous two chapters, these sections do not need to be adhered to rigidly and you may choose from Section A or Section B, or a combination of both, depending on the needs, abilities, and interests of your group. As a facilitator, you can follow the time suggestions for a 50-minute session or spread the session across more than one time period and take longer on the activities, depending on your group.

Session 3, this chapter, is organised in the following format. The aims of the session are outlined, and then the underpinning theoretical approaches and abilities are listed with practical suggestions on how to approach the session (if applicable). Then Section A is presented. The facilitators' toolkit is provided, followed by the introduction. The activities are presented in the following format: a warm up activity; a tuning in activity; the action activity; and then the closure activity. Section A is followed by Section B.

AIMS OF SESSION 3

- Continue to develop skills in working together, taking turns, cooperation, listening to others, and staying on task.

- Continue process of completing autobiographical genogram or Tree of Life and biographical story of the character via genogram or Tree of Life.

- If character genogram is complete, then consider role plays of the character by the participant. Is the character a hero or a villain, a victim to be rescued, a guide, a love interest, the boy/girl next door? Come up with a negotiated scenario and get participants to act out how they might think, feel, and behave.

- Support development of theory of mind via pictorial story, and creative and flexible thinking via extension object substitution activities.

THEORIES, ABILITIES, AND APPROACHES UNDERPINNING SESSION 3

- Person-centred approach.

- Representational thinking through symbolic play (using an object and pretending it is something else).

- Neuro-responsive social scaffolding.

- Theory of mind (problem solving with an extended version of the previous week's theory of mind exercise) (see Chapter 1).

Suggestions for approaching this session

This third session, Session 3, consolidates the atmosphere that you, as a facilitator, created over the past sessions. Your skills as facilitators are critical in setting up a safe, predictable environment where the young person feels warmly welcomed and accepted for who they are. In this session, the participants should be less anxious; however, they will still need predictability in format so that their trust of the facilitators builds on Session 2. You can reflect the unconditional acceptance of your participants and continue to build trust by explaining that in each session the format will be similar, by avoiding asking too many questions of the group, and by ensuring that participants are engaged in the same activities, if appropriate. Be sensitive to when the group comes together as a whole and when participants work on their own or in smaller groups.

SECTION A: FOR MAINSTREAM SCHOOL SETTINGS

FACILITATORS' TOOLKIT

Butchers' paper

Puppets

Characters from modelled clay

Cloth, box, paper plate

Ball of wool or string

Figurines for the theory of mind story

INTRODUCTION

The facilitators welcome the group and provide a verbal outline of the session for the group. One facilitator may give a summary of some of the ideas the group has had about the movie.

WARM UP ACTIVITY (10 MINUTES)

The warm up activity for this session is the Web Game. As the facilitator, you will need a ball of wool or string. You invite the participants to stand in a circle. Once the group is in a circle, you, as the facilitator, hold on to the end of the wool or string and throw the ball to one of the participants to catch. The participant who catches the ball answers a question posed by the other facilitator. Holding the ball, this participant then throws it to another member of the group. This is continued until everyone has had a turn and eventually a web is produced.

Suggested questions to ask the participants are:

1. If you had to leave your house quickly, what three objects would you try and save?
2. If you could talk to any one person, who would it be and why?
3. If you were an animal, what would you be and why?
4. Do you have a pet? If yes, what is your pet? If not, what sort of pet would you like?
5. Name one thing you really like about yourself.
6. What's your favourite thing to do in the holidays?
7. Who is your favourite cartoon character and why?
8. What book, movie, or video that you have seen/read recently would you recommend? Why?
9. What would you like to be/do when you grow up?
10. What's your favourite subject in school?
11. If you could travel anywhere in the world, where would you go?
12. What's your favourite season? Summer? Autumn? Winter? Spring? Why?

TUNING IN ACTIVITY (15 MINUTES)

Symbolic materials game

Part 1: Theory of mind game

If the group easily completed the previous session's theory of mind game (Session 2's activity), then this week includes a similar story with more detail. If your group struggled with the concepts of false belief in last week's theory of mind activities, you might want to go over them again, or use some activities from Section B. Again, you can change your theory of mind story to align with your group's interests, such as including characters from movies or books that the group is familiar with.

As you tell the story, act out the story with the figurines so that your participants are provided with a visual demonstration of the story. As you tell your story, ask questions as you proceed through the story so you can ensure the participants are keeping track of the story. Questions can reflect memory, for example, ""Where was the character when he put the object down?", as well as theory of mind questions, for example, "Where do you think [the character] will go to find [a person/object]?"

To assist facilitators in this activity, the following storyline and questions are provided.

> Sally and Ann lived on a farm. They both liked the rabbit. The rabbit lived in a hutch with a closed door. Sally and Ann looked at the rabbit through the hutch door. Then Sally was called away. Ann loved the rabbit so much she wanted to hold it. So Ann opened the door so she could touch the rabbit and hold it. But the rabbit jumped out and ran away! The rabbit jumped over the fence and lay down underneath a shed. Ann was surprised and then wondered what to do. She closed the hutch door and stood near it. Sally came back. Where did Sally look for the rabbit? Why did Ann close the hutch door?

If participants would like the Sally and Ann game acted out, here is a YouTube link to it:

Sally, Ann, and the rabbit – where does Sally think the rabbit is?

> www.youtube.com/embed/8nxJgsonjYw

Part 2

This activity is an extension to the object substitution (flexible thinking) activity from Session 2. This session's activity incorporates object substitution of three objects, together, to create a new object.

As a facilitator, invite the group to brainstorm what the cloth, box, and paper plate could be used for, and what they could be when used together at the same time. In this activity, the three objects can be three different things within the same scene or the three objects can be one new object. After the group has brainstormed possible alternative uses of the three objects, split the group into two groups. Using some of the ideas that the group came up with, encourage the smaller groups to then work out how the ideas could be used as a part of the movie set.

ACTION ACTIVITY (20 MINUTES)

As a facilitator, you may need to allow time in this action activity for participants to complete the genogram and ecomap or Tree of Life activity for their character from Session 2. If some participants have completed the genogram for their character, then a facilitator can introduce the role-play activity.

Role plays

For this activity, invite participants who have completed their character's genogram (this provides the back-story for their character) to form into pairs. Once they are in pairs, explain to the participants that they are to play out the role of their modelled clay character that they have created. As a facilitator, you may need to brainstorm with the participants so that they understand the sorts of behaviours and feelings they could role play as their character. This activity requires participants to develop a more detailed understanding of their character, and to see the world from their character's point of view. The facilitator may say, "Imagine your character. How would your character feel, how would they act? Is your character a villain? A hero? A guide? A love interest? The person next door?" The facilitator encourages each pair to do a short role play of their character. To extend this activity for those pairs who are gaining a more detailed understanding of their character, the facilitator may suggest narrating a problem or goal of the character the pairs have developed. The facilitator brainstorms, when needed, how to develop understanding of the character the pairs created in order to further develop the narrative surrounding the character.

CLOSURE ACTIVITY (5 MINUTES)

Invite the participants to choose a character from any of this session's activities. That is, they could choose a character from the theory of mind activity or one from the characters they created. Then the participant answers one of the following questions about the character.

1. What do you most like about this character?

2. If this character was coming for dinner at your house, what would you serve them?

3. If you were going to take this character to see something in your town, what would you show them?

4. Who would you most like to introduce your character to in your life?

This closure activity is a reflective finish to the session and a time for the participants to debrief about how they felt about the session and what it was like to "be" their character. When all participants have had a turn (if any participant does not wish to participate, you respect their decision and encourage them to listen to the other participants), ensure that all participants are feeling relaxed and safe. Pack up and finish. Say your goodbyes.

SECTION B: FOR ADOLESCENTS WITH ADDITIONAL NEEDS

Please note the content of Session 3 is delivered over two sessions for Section B. For convenience, the breakdown of Session 3 into two sessions will be referred to as: Session 3 Week 1 and Session 3 Week 2.

FACILITATORS' TOOLKIT

Visual schedule (see Appendix 3)

Box

Paper plate

Piece of cloth

Ball of wool or string

Craft materials

- Rectangular woodblocks
- Glue (adhesive putty)
- Pipe cleaners
- Plastic eyes
- Small pieces of material
- Wool

Two puppets or miniatures

A marble, cup

Prompt cards for commonalities game as used in Session 2 (see Appendix 4)

INTRODUCTION

The facilitator welcomes participants to the session and gives an outline of the session to the participants. You may prefer to use a visual schedule (see Appendix 3).

WARM UP ACTIVITY

Session 3 Week 1 and Week 2

Alternative thinking game with symbolic materials

As the facilitator, present the box (for Session 3 Week 1) or paper plate, piece of cloth and box (for Session 3 Week 2) from your facilitators' toolkit.

For Session 3 Week 1, invite your group to brainstorm and demonstrate alternate uses for the box until no one can think of any more. In Session 3 Week 2, invite the group to brainstorm what the cloth, box, and paper plate could be used for together. Provide time for each participant to respond. Participants may prefer to act out their response and the facilitator can narrate and describe their actions as the participants act it out.

TUNING IN ACTIVITY

Session 3 Week 1 and Week 2

The Web Game

This activity has the same format as that described in Section A. As the facilitator, you will need a ball of wool or string. You invite the participants to stand in a circle. Once the group is in a circle, you, as the facilitator, hold on to the end of the wool and throw the ball to one of the participants to catch. The participant who catches the ball answers a question. Holding the wool, this participant then throws it to another member of the group. This is continued until everyone has had a turn and eventually a web is produced.

Suggested questions to be asked of the participants by the other facilitator are:

1. If your house was burning down, what three objects would you try and save?
2. If you could talk to any one person, who would it be and why?
3. If you were an animal, what would you be and why?
4. Do you have a pet? If yes, what is your pet? If not, what sort of pet would you like?
5. Name one thing you really like about yourself.
6. What's your favourite thing to do in the holidays?
7. Who is your favourite cartoon character and why?
8. What book, movie, or video that you have seen/read recently would you recommend? Why?

9. What would you like to be/do when you grow up?

10. What's your favourite subject in school?

11. If you could travel anywhere in the world, where would you go?

12. What's your favourite season? Summer? Autumn? Winter? Spring? Why?

ACTION ACTIVITY

Session 3 Week 1

Creating Character 2

- The facilitator introduces a woodblock character to the group that the facilitator has made. It has legs, arms, clothes, and hair. The facilitator then discusses the characteristics of the already made model. For example, the woodblock character likes to jump, has a loud voice, and eats ice-cream. The facilitator explains to the group what was needed to make it and why, for example, clothes to keep warm, arms to wave to friends, legs because the character likes jumping, and hair because the character likes to brush it, etc.

- The participants divide into pairs with a staff member allocated to each pair. In pairs, the participants make a character that will later be used in their movie. For the creation of the character, the craft materials from the facilitators' toolkit will be needed. Within the pairs of participants, the staff member facilitates problem solving and brainstorming about what is needed to create the character.

- The facilitator, after checking that all the pairs have completed a character, divides the group into two groups and the participants share their character with other members of the smaller group. Within the two groups, the participants are supported by the facilitator and other staff members to make one comment about what they like about each character.

- The facilitator asks the group to re-form into their pairs. Working in pairs, each participant now draws their character onto their own storyboard and writes down the characteristics of their character. (This information will be used for their story).

- The facilitator points out the similarities and differences between participants and the characters that they created. For example, "Your character really likes playing on a computer tablet, so do you. That is the same", "Your character has crazy, big red hair! You have brown hair. That is different".

Session 3 Week 2
Introduction to theory of mind activity

- The facilitator models a theory of mind false-belief scenario to the group using miniatures or puppets. The facilitator first supports the participants to name miniatures or puppets, then performs the scenario. An example of a theory of mind false-belief scenario could be something like this: Sally puts her marble in a box in the lounge room. Sally leaves the lounge room and goes to another room. While she is gone, Ben comes and takes the marble and puts it in a cup in the lounge room. Sally comes back to get her marble. Where would she look for her marble? In this story, Sally has a false belief about where her marble is. She thinks it is in the box in the lounge room where she left it, but the reader knows that Sally has a false belief about where her marble is, because the reader knows Ben moved the marble to the cup. The facilitator may also prefer to use the short videos from Session 2 Section A.

- After demonstrating the story with the miniatures or puppets, the facilitator asks the group to consider the perspectives of each character by posing questions such as:
  - "Where will Sally look for her marble?"
  - "Why will she look there?"
  - "Why doesn't she know where the marble is?"

- Each participant then has a turn to re-enact the story by leaving the room with the "Sally" puppet/miniature. While "Sally" is out of the room, the facilitator invites the group to hide the marble and repeats the questions above to encourage the group to apply their prior learning. The participant re-enters the room with "Sally" to look for the marble. The facilitator then poses the same questions to the participant who has re-entered the room. "Sally" and the participant will experience the false-belief scenario first-hand and may reflect this to their peers through their words or actions by looking for the marble where they last saw it.

CLOSURE ACTIVITY

Session 3 Week 1 and Week 2

Commonalities

For these sessions, the focus of questions is preferences, likes, and dislikes.

The facilitator invites participants to sit on chairs in a circle. Ensure there is one less chair than there are participants. The facilitator then asks for a volunteer to stand in the middle of the circle and introduce the game to the group, reminding everyone of the rules (that is, a question will be read out, people who have the characteristic in the question stand, then when the signal is given everyone sits down on a different chair). The participant begins the game by posing the first question from the card, for example, Who has black hair? (see Appendix 4). Once all the people who responded positively to the card are standing (for example, those with black hair are standing), the volunteer participant (assisted by the facilitator if needed) draws awareness to the differences between participants' interests and preferences. The volunteer participant then says "Change places, go!" Individuals standing must find another chair in the circle to sit on before the volunteer participant sits. Whoever is left without a chair becomes the new leader. The new leader has a choice between using a visual prompt from the bag or thinking of their own criteria. The game continues until the session time is up or all prompts have been used.

The facilitator may choose other prompt cards if the group indicates they would like to do more or the facilitator may nominate a participant to have a turn.

To finish the session, the facilitator asks participants to share what they enjoyed most. A visual choice board (for instruction on using a visual choice board, see https://youtu.be/fDN6_UUfIHQ; for symbols from the visual schedule, see Appendix 3) may be required to support participants to reflect on the session. Remind participants of the next session and the activities they will do. Pack up and finish.

CHAPTER 6

Session 4: Context, plot structure, props, and scenes

WHAT SHOULD I EXPECT?

Welcome to Session 4. This chapter outlines Session 4 for "Imagine, Create, Belong". Within this chapter, there are two main sections – Section A and Section B. Section A is for young people in their early to mid-adolescence who may be neuro-diverse and attend a mainstream school (Intelligence Quota (IQ) score is greater than or equal to 70). Section B is for young people who have additional needs and attend a special school (for those with an IQ score of less than or equal to 70). In Section B, Session 4 is expanded to cover two sessions across two weeks because young people with additional needs often require more repetition.

As in previous chapters, these sections do not need to be adhered to rigidly and you may choose from Section A or Section B, or a combination of both, depending on the needs, abilities, and interests of your group. You can follow the time suggestions for a 50-minute session or spread the session across more than one time period and take longer on the activities, depending on your group.

In Session 4, this chapter, the facilitator introduces a structure for negotiating the movie plot. The session is organised in the following format. The aims of the session are outlined, then the underpinning theoretical approaches and abilities are listed with practical suggestions on how to approach the session (if applicable). Then Section A is presented. The facilitators' toolkit is provided, followed by the introduction. The activities have the following format: a warm up activity;

a tuning in activity; the action activity; and then the closure activity. Section A is followed by Section B.

AIMS OF SESSION 4

- Build on earlier skills introduced, such as flexible thinking, cooperation, empathy and understanding of other people, and understanding of the self and one's own identity.

- Continue to develop skills in working together, taking turns, listening to others, and staying on task.

- Continue narrative and identity development through considering plot structure from the characters participants have developed. Begin to negotiate storyline structure for six movie scenes.

- Object substitution – more thinking about props and scenes for the movie based on object substitution activities.

THEORIES, ABILITIES, AND APPROACHES UNDERPINNING SESSION 4

- Person-centred approach.

- Representational thinking through symbolic play (using an object and pretending it is something else).

- Neuro-responsive social scaffolding.

- Theory of mind together with social constructivism (using stories from movies or books that are already well known to participants and building on this to develop theory of mind, which requires the participant to take the perspective of another and to answer questions based on what the other person knows) (see Chapter 1).

Suggestions for approaching this session

This fourth session, Session 4, consolidates the atmosphere that you, as a facilitator, have created over the past sessions. By this session, participants should have built trust with the facilitators to provide a safe, predictable environment where the young person feels warmly welcomed and accepted for who they are. In this session, the participants should be much less anxious because now they understand the process and format of the group sessions. You can reflect the unconditional acceptance of your participants by commenting on what you see as the participants' achievements and strengths, for example, "You thought that would be tricky, but you gave it a go and you succeeded". Notice acts of kindness, creativity, generosity, and helpfulness and point these out when appropriate. Work with the participants by demonstrating the activities with them, and reduce the direct questions to the participants, apart from the questions that are embedded in activities.

SECTION A: FOR MAINSTREAM SCHOOL SETTINGS

FACILITATORS' TOOLKIT

- Butchers' paper
- Felt-tip writing pens & adhesive putty
- Blank A4 pieces of paper
- Oven hardening or air drying modelling clay
- Puppets
- Piece of cloth, stick, and some tape

INTRODUCTION

The facilitator welcomes the participants to the session and outlines what will be covered in this session. The facilitator may ask if anyone has any questions or queries from the last session.

WARM UP ACTIVITY (10–15 MINUTES)

Preference game

In this session, the facilitator invites participants to line up, leaving some space between them to allow for movement from side to side. The facilitator calls out questions. In response to the questions, participants decide their answer and show their answer by jumping either left or right depending on what they have decided. For example, in response to the question "Would you rather be invisible or have the power to read minds?", the response of the participant is a jump to the left for invisibility, or a jump to the right for reading minds.

Here are some more options for this activity:

- Would you rather ...?

- For the option of "Would you rather ...?", the facilitator places a line of tape down the centre of the room. The facilitator then asks the group to straddle the tape.

The facilitator explains, "Would you rather?" to the participants, that is, a question will be asked and participants have to jump to the left or right as indicated by the person leading the game. For example, a jump to the right is "doctor" and a jump to the left is "dentist". The facilitator asks if any of the participants would like to lead this game. If yes, then the participant leads the game and the facilitator joins in as one of the group. The leader can change to another participant if there is more than one participant who would like to lead. The questions are:

Would you rather ...?

- Visit the doctor or the dentist?

- Eat broccoli or carrots?

- Watch TV or listen to music?

- Own a lizard or a snake?

- Have a beach holiday or a mountain holiday?

- Be an apple or a banana?

- Be invisible or be able to read minds?

- Be hairy all over or completely bald?

- Be the most popular or the smartest person you know?

- Make headlines for saving somebody's life or winning a Nobel Prize?
- Go without television or fast food for the rest of your life?
- Always be cold or always be hot?
- Not hear or not see?
- Eliminate hunger and disease or be able to bring lasting world peace?
- Be stranded on a deserted island alone or with someone you don't like?
- See the future or change the past?
- Be 3 inches taller or 3 inches shorter?
- Wrestle a lion or fight a shark?

TUNING IN ACTIVITY (10 MINUTES)

Theory of mind (5 minutes)

The facilitator prepares a narrative that the group is familiar with. For example, from previous sessions, the facilitator should have some idea of what movies, stories, or hobbies are of interest to participants in the group. Using a story that the participants have an interest in, you, as facilitator, devise an original story (not a script that the group is already aware of) along the lines of the theory of mind script below and use figurines to act it out as you tell the story.

In this session, the main questions are about what Character 1 thought about Character 2 and where Character 2 was going or doing, and why they thought that.

> **The skate park**
> Bailey loved his skateboard. He was playing on his skateboard in the lane near his house. John came along and wanted to skate too, but didn't have a skateboard. Bailey wouldn't give John a turn so John suggested he could get his GoPro® (action camera)

from home and film Bailey. Sam was there too and had a skateboard but the wheel broke. Bailey told John that he would be skating in the lane all day. John went home to get his GoPro and Sam went home to get a new wheel. After John and Sam left, Bailey changed his mind; he decided to go to the skate park as it was more exciting skating there. On the way to the skate park, Bailey saw Sam and told Sam he was going to the skate park. John got his GoPro® and went back to Bailey's house. John saw Bailey's dad on the footpath near Bailey's house and said "Where's Bailey?" Bailey's dad said, "Bailey's skating". Where does John think Bailey is skating? Why? Where does Sam think Bailey is skating? Why?

For another version of a similar story use the link below:

Bailey, Sam, Liam – where does Sam think the boys are skating?

www.youtube.com/embed/VM2iefh0fJA

Representational thinking with symbolic materials game (5 minutes)

The facilitator introduces a cloth and a stick and leads the group in brainstorming on alternate uses for a cloth and a stick until no one can think of any more.

ACTION ACTIVITY (30 MINUTES – INCLUDE BREAK IF NEEDED)

The role plays from Session 3 are carried over to this session in case your group needs more time to complete this action activity or needs more time to understand how they would role play their character. If your group is ready to do something further, then skip the role plays and move on to the plot structure development.

Role plays

For this activity, invite participants who have completed their character's genogram or Tree of Life (this provides the back-story for their character) to form into pairs. Once they are in pairs, explain to the participants that they play out the role of the modelled clay character that they have created. As a facilitator, you may need to brainstorm with the participants so that they understand the sorts of behaviours and feelings they could role play as their character. This activity requires more detailed understanding of the character from the character's point of view. The facilitator may say, "Imagine your character. How would your character feel, how would they act? Is your character a villain? A hero? A guide? A love interest? The person next door?" The facilitator encourages each pair to do a short role play of their character. To extend this activity for those pairs who are gaining a more detailed understanding of their character, the facilitator may suggest narrating a problem or goal of the character the pairs have developed. The facilitator brainstorms, when needed, how to develop understanding of the character the pairs created in order to develop the narrative surrounding the character further.

Plot structure development

The action activity in Session 4 is to continue with the development of the participants' characters but within the narrative of the movie. By this session, the facilitator starts negotiating the various narratives that the group has raised in the previous sessions. This is not an easy task and requires the facilitator to be responsive to the group's ideas so that all participants feel that their ideas are being included. The facilitator will need to be creative. To assist participants to refine their ideas, the following activities are revisited or extended.

1. Review the genograms and ecomaps or Tree of Life of the characters. The facilitator reminds the group of the genogram and ecomap or Tree of Life that they developed for their characters. The facilitator invites the group to decide on the characters they want in the

movie and to revisit their genograms and ecomaps or Tree of Life to see if there is any further detail they would like to add.

2. The facilitator introduces a storyline structure guide with six movie scenes (use butchers' paper as storyboards because this gives more space for writing and drawings and allows the whole group to see what is on the paper). The plot structure is a guide for the group in how to structure the movie plot. However, the context of the story may shift and be fluid. For adolescents who are neuro-diverse, memory is an issue and holding multiple concepts in mind at the same time is challenging. A movie plot has multiple concepts, such as: character actions; what characters say; what props are needed; interactions between characters; what will happen next in the plot. As a facilitator, be prepared for the group to negotiate the movie plot in the moment, that is, expect more improvisation in the moment than planned storylines. At this stage, the movie plot will not be cohesive; however, the facilitator can describe to the group what ideas have been put forward by the group and open the discussion on how these ideas can join together into one movie. To aid in this process, the movie plot can be broken down into six movie scenes. The facilitator, using butchers' paper so the whole group can see what is written, divides the paper into six areas. The facilitator discusses that one scene would be the beginning of the movie and the sixth scene would be the end of the movie. Discussion is opened up in the group as to the possible beginnings and endings of the movie plot (narrative). Depending on the group, the facilitator then works with the group to fill in the remaining four scenes and what will possibly happen as the story unfolds.

3. Develop plot further. Once the group has decided and negotiated what is possible in the six scenes, then the facilitator begins to support the group with further script development. For example, which character will say what and when in the movie? How will the characters interact/act? For example, who will be friends, who will be enemies? Allow time for the participants to add in ideas on how their characters will interact. As a facilitator, expect this process to be fluid within the group.

4. Character development. The participants are starting to understand how their character could contribute to the movie plot. To support this, the facilitator invites participants to develop their individual modelled clay characters (and puppet characters, if used) further. For example, can characters be the villain, the hero, the sidekick, the love interest, the guide, and so on? How do they interact with some characters and differently with others?

CLOSURE ACTIVITY (5 MINUTES)

Session 4 requires a large amount of time for the action activity. For closure, the facilitator may visit the representational thinking with symbolic materials game (see Session 2, p. 57, and Session 3, p. 71) and guide the group to consider how some of the ideas thought of earlier in the group session could be incorporated as props and scenes into the movie plot.

When time is up or the facilitator perceives that the group has worked hard and needs to finish, pack up and finish. Say your goodbyes.

SECTION B: FOR ADOLESCENTS WITH ADDITIONAL NEEDS

Please note the content of Session 4 is delivered over two sessions for Section B. For convenience, the breakdown of Session 4 into two sessions will be referred to as: Session 4 Week 1 and Session 4 Week 2.

FACILITATORS' TOOLKIT

Visual schedule (see Appendix 3)

Set of "goal" and "problem" cards (see Appendix 7)

Puppets and woodblock characters

Access to video *Knick Knack* (https://youtu.be/9uhM_SUhdaw)

Blank storyboard sheet

Participant storyboards

Cut and paste pictures for activity

Paper and glue

INTRODUCTION

The facilitator welcomes the participants to the session and outlines what will be covered in this session. The facilitator may use a visual schedule (see Appendix 3).

WARM UP ACTIVITY

Session 4 Week 1 and Week 2

Postcards

- The facilitator has prepared a set of "goal" and "problem" cards (see Appendix 7 for ideas) and places them in a bag, ready for the session. The facilitator invites each member of the group to pick a card out of a bag. There are two of each card and each card has either a "goal" or a "problem". Once participants have picked their card from the bag, they then find their partner by matching their cards. That is, the "goal" card is matched to the "problem" card.

- Once the participants have found their partner, they then work in pairs with a staff member. In pairs, the participants discuss which picture is a goal and which picture is a problem.

TUNING IN ACTIVITY

Session 4 Week 1

The facilitator invites the participants to bring the characters they made in the last session and to introduce them to the group. In introducing their character to the group, the facilitator prompts the participant (if needed) to provide the character's name and, using the character's voice, to talk about things the character likes or does not like.

Session 4 Week 2

The facilitator plays a short engaging video clip (for example, Pixar's *Knick Knack*) and then models story development using the storyboard (see Appendix 1) based on the short clip. This activity was also carried out in Session 1 Week 1 (Chapter 3, Action activity, p. 49). This activity is repeated, with the participants leading discussion regarding characters, goal, problem, solutions, and conclusion. The facilitator or a volunteer participant writes down the suggestions from the group onto a blank storyboard template. The facilitator then summarises the discussion for the group.

ACTION ACTIVITY

Session 4 Week 1

Goals and problems

- In this session, the facilitator reviews the storyboards with the group. The facilitator presents the storyboard that was created in Session 1 Week 1 to reflect on the storyboard process. The facilitator explains that, "This week we are going to look at these parts – goals and problems. A goal is something that we want to do, like ride the bikes. A problem is something that stops us from doing what we want to do, like if the bike shed was locked". Explain the goal and problem from the initial storyboard.

- The facilitator plays a short clip of a popular movie or short film (for example, Pixar's *Presto*) for the group to watch. After the group watches the clip, the group creates a storyboard with the participants identifying Characters 1 and 2, the goal, problem, solution, and conclusion of the story. This is supported by the facilitator where needed. The facilitator then divides the group into two groups. With reference to the short clip *Presto*, half of the group focuses on the goal of the magician, and the other half of the group focuses on the goal of the rabbit.

- The facilitator compares and contrasts the goals of the magician with those of the rabbit and invites discussion from the group, if appropriate.

- Participants are then invited to break into pairs with a staff member. They complete a sorting activity with a range of "goals" and "problems" (see cards from Appendix 7), pasting them into two columns (goal/problem). By repeating this activity with this variation, the participants' understanding of goals and problems is reinforced.

- The facilitator invites participants to move from their pairs to two small groups and talk about any problems or goal cards they were not sure about. Facilitator and staff members give explanations for any issues that the participants raise.

Session 4 Week 2

- Revisit completed sorting activity worksheets with the range of goals and problems from the Session 4 Week 1 (p. 90). After this activity, the group breaks into small groups (one facilitator with each group) and moves to tables.

- Goal writing: the facilitator hands out participants' characters from previous sessions (puppet and woodblock) and storyboards. The facilitator explains that participants need to think of a goal for their characters, that is, something they really want to do. Invite the participants to draw this goal onto the storyboards.

- Problem writing: the facilitator says, "Now we need to think of a problem, something that will stop your characters from reaching their goal". The facilitator invites the participants to draw this problem onto the storyboards.

- The group then moves into pairs. In the pairs, the participants retell the story of the character's goal and problem within their pairs.

CLOSURE ACTIVITY

Session 4 Week 1 and Week 2

Commonalities game

For these sessions, the focus of questions is preferences, likes, and dislikes.

The facilitator invites participants to sit on chairs in a circle. Ensure there is one less chair than there are participants. The facilitator then asks for a volunteer to stand in the middle of the circle and introduce the game to the group, reminding everyone of the rules (see Session 3). The participant begins the game by posing the first question from the card (see Appendix 4). Once all the people who responded positively to the card are standing (for example, those who like cake are standing), the volunteer participant (assisted by the facilitator if needed) draws awareness to the differences between participants' interests and preferences. The volunteer participant then directs, "Change places, go!" Individuals standing must find another chair in the circle to sit on before the volunteer participant sits. Whoever is left without a chair becomes the new leader. The new leader has a choice between using a visual prompt from the bag or thinking of their own criteria. The game continues until the session time is up or all prompts have been used.

Ask participants to share what they enjoyed most. A visual choice board (for instruction on using a visual choice board, see https://youtu.be/fDN6_UUfIHQ; for symbols from the visual schedule, see Appendix 3) may be required to support participants to reflect on the session. Remind participants of the next session and the activities they will do. Pack up and finish.

CHAPTER 7

Session 5: Beginning to identify problems to solve in the story

WHAT SHOULD I EXPECT?

Welcome to Session 5. This chapter outlines Session 5 for "Imagine, Create, Belong". Within this chapter, there are two main sections – Section A and Section B. Section A is for young people in their early to mid-adolescence who may be neuro-diverse and attend a mainstream school (Intelligence Quota (IQ) score is greater than or equal to 70). Section B is for young people who have additional needs and attend a special school (for those with an IQ score of less than or equal to 70). In Section B, Session 5 is expanded to cover two sessions across two weeks because young people with additional needs require more time to process the skills and concepts.

As in previous chapters, these sections do not need to be adhered to rigidly and you may choose from Section A or Section B, or a combination of both, depending on the needs, abilities, and interests of your group. You can follow the time suggestions for a 57-minute session or spread the session across more than one time period and take longer on the activities, depending on your group.

Session 5, this chapter, is organised in the following format. The aims of the session are outlined, then the underpinning theoretical approaches and abilities are listed with practical suggestions on how to approach the session (if applicable). Then Section A is presented. The facilitators' toolkit is provided, followed by the introduction. The activities have the following format: a warm up activity; a tuning in activity; the action activity; and then the closure activity. Section A is followed by Section B.

AIMS OF SESSION 5

- Continue to develop skills in working together, taking turns, listening to others, and staying on task.

- Build on earlier skills introduced, such as flexible thinking, cooperation, empathy and understanding of other people, and understanding of the self and one's own identity.

- Main activity is in small groups to continue negotiating problems to solve.

- To bring the group closer to a negotiated narrative within the movie plot with attention to the characters. Flexible thinking is encouraged through alternative uses for objects used in substitution.

THEORIES, ABILITIES, AND APPROACHES UNDERPINNING SESSION 5

- Person-centred approach.

- Representational thinking through symbolic play (using an object and pretending it is something else).

- Neuro-responsive social scaffolding.

- Theory of mind (problem solving with an extended version of the previous week's theory of mind exercise).

- Negotiated narrative develops further (see Chapter 1).

Suggestions for approaching this session

This fifth session, Session 5, has a predictable, friendly atmosphere that you, as a facilitator, have created over the past sessions. By this session, participants should have built trust with the facilitator to provide a safe, predictable environment where the young person feels warmly welcomed and accepted for who they are. In this session, the participants now understand the process and format of the group sessions. You can reflect the unconditional acceptance of your participants by commenting on what you see as the participants' achievements, for example, "You thought about how your character would do that and now you have a solution". Work with the participants by demonstrating the activities alongside them and reduce the direct questions to the participants, apart from the questions that are embedded in activities.

SECTION A: FOR MAINSTREAM SCHOOL SETTINGS

FACILITATORS' TOOLKIT

Butchers' paper

Puppets

Modelled clay characters

Cloth, box, paper plate

Ball of wool or string

INTRODUCTION (2 MINUTES)

The facilitator welcomes the participants to the session and outlines what will be covered in this session. The facilitator may ask if anyone has any questions or queries from the last session.

WARM UP ACTIVITY (5 MINUTES)

The warm up activity this session is the Web Game. The facilitator will need a ball of wool or string. The facilitator invites the participants to stand in a circle. The facilitator holds onto the end of the string and throws the ball to one of the participants to catch. After the participant catches the ball, they then answer a question. Holding the string, the participant then throws it to another member of the group, and so on, until everyone has had a turn. Eventually a web is produced.

The questions asked of participants as they catch the ball are given below. Each participant is asked one question, unless the group wants to keep going and answer more than one question each.

1. If you had to leave your house quickly, what three objects would you try and save?
2. If you could talk to any one person now living, who would it be and why?
3. If you were an animal, what would you be and why?
4. Do you have a pet? If not, what sort of pet would you like?
5. Name one thing you really like about yourself.
6. What's your favourite thing to do in the holidays?
7. Who is your favourite cartoon character and why?
8. What book, movie, or video have you seen/read recently that you would recommend? Why?
9. What would you like to be/do when you grow up?
10. What's your favourite subject in school?
11. If you could travel anywhere in the world, where would you go?
12. What's your favourite season? Summer? Autumn? Winter? Spring? Why?

TUNING IN ACTIVITY (20–25 MINUTES)

Theory of mind game (10–15 minutes)

If the group has easily completed the previous week's theory of mind game, then this week a harder version can be delivered. If the group found the theory of mind game in Session 4 difficult, repeat the theory of mind story game, with a variation of the characters. The variation of the characters could include characters of different gender, name, age, and profession. The story details are then varied to be consistent with the change in characters.

If the group is ready for a harder version of the theory of mind game, a suggested story is given below. This story includes the concept of bluffing and is based on theory of mind stories from Liddle and Nettle (2006). Again, you can change the narrative to align with your group's interests. The facilitator may use figurines as they tell the story. This gives a visual understanding of what is happening in the story. The facilitator asks participants questions as the story develops to ensure that the participants are keeping track of the story. That is, ask questions related to memory as well as theory of mind questions.

> Susan and Bill are in the same class at school for English. They have been working very hard and so their teacher, Mrs Anderson, suggests that next week they could bring along a video to watch. Mrs Anderson suggests they bring something that she would also like. Susan likes movies that have adventure stories and Bill likes crime mysteries. Susan has no idea what movies Mrs Anderson likes. Bill comes to talk to Susan and they both agree they would like to bring in a movie. Bill asks Susan what movies Mrs Anderson likes. Susan suggests that Mrs Anderson likes adventure movies. Bill thinks about this and then agrees that Susan should bring an adventure movie next week to class.

- Memory questions: Who is Mrs Anderson? What did she say to Susan and Bill? What movies does Susan like? What movies does Bill like?
- Theory of mind questions: Why did Susan say Mrs Anderson likes adventure movies? Why would Bill agree with Susan? How would Susan feel about Bill agreeing with her about Mrs Anderson's movie choice?

Representational thinking through symbolic materials game (10 minutes)

As the facilitator, present the cloth, box, and paper plate to the group. As a group, brainstorm what the cloth, box, and paper plate could be if they were used together. Potentially split the group into two groups. One group could brainstorm how to use the objects as one object and the other group could brainstorm how the three objects could be used in relation to each other. After the groups have come up with some ideas, the facilitator turns the brainstorming to how the ideas could be used as a part of the movie set.

ACTION ACTIVITY (15–20 MINUTES)

Role plays

The facilitator invites the group to split into smaller groups of three or four. The facilitator encourages the participants to include a problem in the role play that their character will need to overcome. The facilitator may also suggest that participants think about how the problem could be solved, if the group would not be too overwhelmed. The aim of this action activity is for participants to gain a deeper understanding of the negotiated plot for the movie and a more in-depth understanding of each character's role. The facilitator explains that in this session the participants can refer back to the collaborative six movie scenes plot structure from the last session. The movie plot is being developed by the group. The facilitator then supports the smaller groups to devise short role plays with the puppet characters and/or modelled clay characters that includes a problem for the character.

The facilitator may prompt the participants to assist them in ideas for the role plays. For example, the facilitator may suggest ideas for problems that come from movies, the participants' own lives, or previous ideas raised in the group. The main outcome of this session is for participants to have negotiated plots and sub-plots around the problem. In the short role plays, the smaller groups of participants will be practising working together, taking turns, listening to others, staying on task. The facilitator observes the groups and wanders from group to group supporting interactions where needed. For example, the facilitator may need to summarise the ideas of the small groups to give a better understanding to the group of the ideas they have so far.

CLOSURE ACTIVITY (5 MINUTES)

For the closure activity, the facilitator brings the whole group together. The facilitator opens a discussion about which character problems the participants related to the most. This is a reflective activity for the group. As an extension activity, the facilitator can invite the group to discuss what message might be conveyed by the story that is coming to life. Is it about courage, loyalty, determination, or something else? The facilitator ensures that all participants leave the group feeling supported and safe.

Pack up and finish. Say your goodbyes.

SECTION B: ADOLESCENTS WITH ADDITIONAL NEEDS

Please note the content of Session 5 is delivered over two sessions for Section B. For convenience, the breakdown of Session 5 into two sessions will be referred to as: Session 5 Week 1 and Session 5 Week 2.

FACILITATORS' TOOLKIT

Visual schedule (see Appendix 3)

4–6 inanimate objects (such as bottle top, box, cloth, pen, paper plate, CD, cardboard tube)

Miniatures/puppets

Marble

Goal and problem cut and paste sheets from Session 4

Knick Knack storyboard. See https://YouTu.be/9uhM_SUhdaw to revise the story

Participants' storyboards

INTRODUCTION

The facilitator welcomes the participants to the session and outlines what will be covered in this session. The facilitator may use a visual schedule (see Appendix 3).

WARM UP ACTIVITY

Session 5 Week 1 and Week 2

Object stories introduction

The facilitator invites the participants to choose two to three items from a selection of four to six. The facilitator lets the participants know that the items will be used in the creation of a short story. The facilitator supports the participants to choose the items, such as a bottle top, box, and cloth. The facilitator then supports the participants to act out or narrate a short sequence using the items.

The facilitator provides an example for the group, for instance, a person (bottle top) swimming in a lake (blue cloth) or a person (bottle top) driving a car (box).

When the participants have all had a turn at creating a narrative from the items, the facilitator moves on to the theory of mind game.

TUNING IN ACTIVITY

Session 5 Week 1 and Week 2

Theory of mind (review and consolidation)

- The facilitator models a theory of mind scenario for the whole group using miniatures or puppets. The theory of mind scenario goes something like: Sally puts her marble in a box in the lounge room. She leaves the room. While she is away, Ben comes in and sees the marble and he moves it to a bag. Sally comes back to get her marble. Where does she look for her marble?

- The facilitator then invites the group to name the two characters from the story they have just seen. The facilitator asks the group to consider the perspectives of each character by posing questions such as:

  - "Where did Sally put her marble?"
  - "Where will Sally look for her marble?"
  - "Why will she look there?"
  - "Why doesn't she know where the marble is?"

- The story is then re-enacted with the participants themselves. Each participant places the marble somewhere in the room, while holding the "Ben" puppet and then leaves the room with the "Sally" puppet. While "Sally" is out of the room, the facilitator invites the group to hide the marble in another place and repeats the questions above to encourage the group to apply their prior learning. The facilitator then invites the participant to re-enter with "Sally" to look for the marble. The facilitator then poses the same questions to the participant who has re-entered the room.

- This activity is repeated from Session 3 (p. 77) to ensure the majority of participants have an opportunity to build and consolidate their understanding of the concept. Some participants may grasp the concept early and can act as supports for their peers who require multiple exposures.

ACTION ACTIVITY
Session 5 Week 1

The facilitator plays the short video *Knick Knack* to the group for review. The facilitator then continues with the following activities.

- Storyboard. The facilitator takes the group through a review of the *Knick Knack* video and storyboard from Session 1, paying particular attention to the solution and conclusion of the story.

- With the group, the facilitator reviews the goal and problem cut and paste sheet from Session 4. The facilitator then brainstorms possible solutions with the group (that is, something that fixes the problem) and possible conclusions (that is, what is the result of your solution?).

    - For example, a goal could be: I really want to ride the bike. The problem is: the bike shed is locked. The possible solution is: I ask my teacher to unlock the shed. The conclusion is: I get to ride the bike, I feel happy.

    - After reviewing the storyboard and the goal and problem sheets, the participants form into pairs and revisit the goal and problem sheet from Session 4 and discuss and add solutions and conclusions to the story.

- The facilitator instructs the pairs to form two small groups and talk about anything they were not sure about – if your group is short on time, skip this step.

- The facilitator organises the smaller groups into two groups. The participants review their own storyboard, including the character, goal, and problem. Participants are encouraged by the facilitator to think of their story and then add their own solution and conclusion to the storyboard.

Session 5 Week 2

This action activity follows directly from Session 5 Week 1. The participants continue to review their own storyboard, paying particular attention to the following.

- With the group, the facilitator reviews the goal and problem cut and paste sheet, including solutions and conclusions from Session 5 Week 1.

- The facilitator invites participants to review their own storyboard, character, goal, and problem. The participants brainstorm and add their own solutions and conclusions to their storyboard.

CLOSURE ACTIVITY

Session 5 Week 1 and Week 2

Commonalities game

For these sessions, the focus of questions is preferences, likes, and dislikes.

The facilitator invites participants to sit on chairs in a circle. Ensure there is one less chair than there are participants. The facilitator then asks for a volunteer to stand in the middle of the circle and introduce the game to the group, reminding everyone of the rules (see previous sessions). The participant begins the game by posing the first question from a card (see Appendix 4). Once all the people who responded positively to the card are standing (for example, those who like cake are standing), the volunteer participant (assisted by the facilitator if needed) draws awareness to the differences between participants' interests and preferences. The volunteer participant then directs "Change places, go!" Individuals standing must find another chair in the circle to sit on before the volunteer participant sits. Whoever is left without a chair becomes the new leader. The new leader has a choice between using a visual prompt from the cards in the bag or thinking of their own criteria. The game continues until the session time is up or all prompts have been used.

Ask participants to share what they enjoyed most. A visual choice board (for instruction on using a visual choice board, see https://youtu.be/fDN6_UUfIHQ; for symbols from the visual schedule, see Appendix 3) may be required to support participants to reflect on the session. Remind participants of the next session and the activities they will do. Pack up and finish.

REFERENCE

Liddle, B., & Nettle, D. (2006). Higher-order theory of mind and social competence in school-age children. *Journal of Cultural and Evolutionary Psychology*, 4, 230–244. doi: 10.1556/JCEP.4.2006.3-4.3

CHAPTER 8

Session 6: How will the characters solve the identified problems and what are the props for the movie?

WHAT SHOULD I EXPECT?

Welcome to Session 6. This chapter outlines Session 6 for "Imagine, Create, Belong". Within this chapter, there are two main sections – Section A and Section B. Section A is for young people in their early to mid-adolescence who may be neuro-diverse and attend a mainstream school (Intelligence Quota (IQ) score is greater than or equal to 70). Section B is for young people who have additional needs and attend a special school (for those with an IQ score of less than or equal to 70). In Section B, Session 6 is expanded to cover two sessions across two weeks because young people with additional needs require more time to process the skills and concepts.

As in previous chapters, these sections do not need to be adhered to rigidly and you may choose from Section A or Section B, or a combination of both, depending on the needs, abilities, and interests of your group. You can follow the time suggestions for a 45-minute session or spread the session across more than one time period and take longer on the activities, depending on your group.

Session 6, this chapter, is organised in the following format. The aims of the session are outlined, then the underpinning theoretical approaches and abilities are listed with practical suggestions on how to approach the session (if applicable). Then Section A is presented.

The facilitators' toolkit is provided, followed by how the facilitator introduces Session 6. The activities have the following format: a warm up activity; a tuning in activity; the action activity; and then the closure activity. Section A is followed by Section B.

AIMS OF SESSION 6

- Continue to develop skills in working together, taking turns, listening to others, and staying on task.

- Continue to bring closer a negotiated narrative within the movie with attention focused on the problem and the resolution to the problem in the story. Flexible thinking is challenged through a more complex activity using object substitution.

THEORIES, ABILITIES, AND APPROACHES UNDERPINNING SESSION 6

- Person-centred approach.

- Representational thinking through symbolic play (using an object and pretending it is something else) within a narrative.

- Neuro-responsive social scaffolding.

- Theory of mind within a narrative (problem solving for a character within a story) (see Chapter 1).

Suggestions for approaching this session

This sixth session, Session 6, has a predictable, friendly atmosphere that you, as a facilitator, have created over past sessions. Participants should have built trust with the facilitator to provide a safe, predictable environment where the young person feels warmly welcomed and accepted for who they are. The participants know the process and format of the group sessions. You can reflect the unconditional acceptance of your participants by commenting on what you see as the participants' achievements, for example, "You have been thinking about that for a long time. I wonder what solution you have thought about". Continue to make a point of noticing participants' strengths and talents and drawing attention to these to ensure they feel valued for who they are and what they bring to the group. Neuro-diverse young people, while not a homogenous group, may have particular abilities and strengths not seen as often among neuro-typical groups the same age. Examples include, but are not limited to, thinking about topics in original and fresh ways; thinking deeply about topics; being able to focus on and remember details about topics they are interested in; being helpful, kind, honest, and generous; maintaining independent thought even when in a group. Work with the participants by demonstrating the activities, and reduce the direct questions to the participants, apart from the questions that are embedded in activities.

SECTION A: FOR MAINSTREAM SCHOOL SETTINGS

FACILITATORS' TOOLKIT

Butchers' paper

Whiteboard

Whiteboard markers

Objects collected and placed in a dark coloured bag – the objects can include everyday items, for example, a pencil, key-ring, mobile phone, but also some more unusual ones, such as a fossil, holiday photograph, or wig!

INTRODUCTION

The facilitator welcomes the participants to the session and outlines what will be covered in this session. The facilitator may ask if anyone has any questions or queries from the last session.

WARM UP ACTIVITY (5 MINUTES)
Object stories

This activity is an extension of the object substitution activities because this time the objects need to be incorporated into a narrative. The facilitator has collected together several objects and placed them in a canvas or dark coloured bag.

The facilitator passes the bag around the group and invites each young person to dip their hand into the bag (without looking) and pull out one of the objects. The facilitator explains that the objects that have been chosen need to be included in a story. The facilitator or one of the participants (depending on your group) begins a story which includes the object. If your group needs more assistance with narrative, then the facilitator should begin the story with the objects first. If your group can initiate a story, then ask if someone would like to start. The first person speaks for about 20 seconds, beginning a story that includes the object they have taken from the bag. Then, the next person in the group takes up the story and adds another 20 seconds, incorporating the object they are holding. This continues until everyone has contributed to the epic literary tale! Let imaginations run wild! Encourage the group to move the story beyond their everyday experience.

TUNING IN ACTIVITY (15 MINUTES)
Problem to solve activity

In this activity, the facilitator encourages the participants to think of a joint small "problem to solve" for their characters. The group needs to come up with an agreed problem and solution. The problem also needs to feed into the movie plot thus far. Support may be needed from the facilitator for the group to come up with an agreed problem and solution. Some ideas the facilitator can offer the group are given below. From time to time, the facilitator may need to summarise the ideas so far so the group has a concept of where the discussion is going and if the group is closer to an agreed idea for the problem and solution.

The problem can be simple; however, some ideas are listed here:

- The character needs to reach a goal but there is a problem stopping them. What is the problem? (The facilitator could take an example from the Harry Potter or *The Hunger Games* books/movies) What is the solution?

- The problem is the mystery. What is the mystery? (The facilitator could take an example from *Scooby-Doo* or Harry Potter.) What is the solution?

- The characters need to complete a journey. What is a problem on the way? (The facilitator could take an example from *Star Wars*®.) What is the solution?

- There is a problem that causes the characters to flee or pursue. What is the problem? (The facilitator could take an example from *The Maze*.) What is the solution?

- The problem is a change in the character as the character develops a new power. What do you do with your new power?

- The problem could be something to do with growing up or personal growth; for example, the character grows taller or the character's voice changes. What is the solution?

ACTION ACTIVITY (20 MINUTES – TAKE BREAK IF NEEDED)

The action activity follows on from where the group finished in Session 5. This session continues with development of the negotiated movie plot (narrative) . In this session, the focus is on the problem and the solution in the narrative.

The facilitator hands out butchers' paper to the group. Alternatively, if a whiteboard is available, the facilitator may choose to use the whiteboard. On the paper or whiteboard, the facilitator outlines the movie script so far. Or the facilitator brings out notes from the previous session, where the group's shared ideas are listed. The following steps are the outline for the action activity in this session.

1. The movie script. The ideas on the butchers' paper or whiteboard are reviewed by the group. The facilitator is aiming to have a negotiated movie script by bringing together all the different ideas that the group has put forward over the previous sessions. Your group may have a negotiated script by now or your group may still need more work. If your group has not come to the point where the movie narrative is starting to come together, then use this session to focus on this – a negotiated movie plot. The focus of this session is adding the problem and resolution into the storyboard. For the problem to be included, point out to the group it may affect all or some of the characters. Give all participants an opportunity to write or draw on the board or butchers' paper what they perceive as a problem for the character in the movie plot.

2. After all participants have contributed to the problem and resolution within the negotiated movie plot, the facilitator reviews with the group how the movie has progressed thus far.

3. As part of this session, the facilitator also includes in the discussion the scenery, props, music, and sound effects that may also be needed for the movie. Many of these ideas would have been raised in past sessions. The facilitator reminds the group of what ideas have been put forward.

4. The facilitator reminds participants that there are only two sessions left and that in the last session the group will be making the movie and it will be recorded so all the participants can have a copy.

CLOSURE ACTIVITY (5 MINUTES)

In the closure activity, the facilitator opens a discussion by asking, "Is there a movie you really liked?", "Is there a movie you really don't like?", and "Which movie have you seen that inspired you the most?"

This activity is a reflective activity for the participants to think about what they like and do not like in a movie. After the discussion, the group packs up and finishes. Say your goodbyes.

SECTION B: ADOLESCENTS WITH ADDITIONAL NEEDS

Please note the content of Session 6 is delivered over two sessions for Section B. For convenience, the breakdown of Session 6 into two sessions will be referred to as: Session 6 Week 1 and Session 6 Week 2.

FACILITATORS' TOOLKIT

Visual schedule (see Appendix 3)

Opaque bag with items for object stories (for example, squeeze ball, plastic plate, toy cars, empty milk drink carton, CD, cardboard tube)

Participant storyboards

Craft materials/items identified by participants to make their props

INTRODUCTION

The facilitator welcomes the participants to the session and outlines what will be covered in this session. The facilitator may use a visual schedule (see Appendix 3).

WARM UP AND TUNING IN ACTIVITY

Session 6 Week 1 and Week 2

Object stories

The warm up activity is similar to that in Section A. However, the facilitator will need to give additional time and scaffolding for the participants to complete the activity. Facilitators check in and summarise the story thus far, following each participant's contribution. This supports individuals with a poor memory who require a longer processing time.

This activity is an extension of the object substitution activities because this time the objects need to be incorporated into a narrative. The facilitator has collected together several objects and placed them in a canvas or dark coloured bag.

The facilitator passes the bag around the group and invites each young person to dip their hand into the bag (without looking) and pull out one of the objects. The facilitator explains that the objects that have been chosen need to be included in a story. If your group needs more assistance with narrative, then the facilitator begins the story with their object first. The first person to begin the activity uses the object in a story. Then, the next person in the group takes up the story and adds to the story, incorporating the object they are holding. The facilitator reviews the story between each participant's additions to the story. This continues until everyone has contributed to the story. Encourage the group to move the story beyond their everyday experience.

ACTION ACTIVITY

Prop design

Session 6 Week 1

Supported by the facilitator and staff members, the participants, who are in pairs, review their storyboards and brainstorm the props that will be required to film their story. The facilitator writes a list of the required props and ideas for craft materials that will be needed to construct props in the following session.

Session 6 Week 2

The facilitator has collected the materials needed to make the props. The participants choose from the provided craft materials what they need to construct the props for the movie.

Please note, in both weeks facilitator and staff support will be needed to support participants to generate self-initiated ideas for the props. This support is given using least-to-most fading, where the teacher "allows the learner a brief opportunity to respond independently on each training trial and then delivers the least intrusive prompt if needed" (Libby, Weiss, Bancroft, & Ahearn, 2008). Thus, after a least intrusive prompt is given, more support may be needed, so an increasingly directive approach in generating ideas for props using provided materials may be used.

For example, the facilitator could say: "I wonder what we could do to this box to turn it into a castle? Let's look at this picture of a castle, it appears to have a door and windows." Provide processing time with an expectant pause to demonstrate to the participant that they can provide a response.

CLOSURE ACTIVITY

Session 6 Week 1 and Week 2

Commonalities game

For these sessions, the focus of questions is preferences, likes, and dislikes.

The facilitator invites participants to sit on chairs in a circle. Ensure there is one less chair than there are participants. The facilitator then asks for a volunteer to stand in the middle of the circle and introduce the game to the group, reminding everyone of the rules (see previous sessions). The participant begins the game by posing the first question from the card (see Appendix 4). Once all the people who responded positively to the card are standing (for example, those who like cake are standing), the volunteer participant (assisted by the facilitator if needed) draws awareness to the differences between participants' interests and preferences. The volunteer participant then directs "Change places, go!" Individuals standing must find another chair in the circle to sit on before the volunteer participant sits. Whoever is left without a chair becomes the new leader. The new leader has a choice between using a visual prompt from the bag or thinking of their own criteria. The game continues until the session time is up or all prompts have been used.

Ask participants to share what they enjoyed most. A visual choice board (for instruction on using a visual choice board, see https://youtu.be/fDN6_UUfIHQ; symbols from the visual schedule, see Appendix 3) may be required to support participants to reflect on the session. Remind participants of the next session and the activities they will do. Pack up and finish.

REFERENCE

Libby, M. E., Weiss, J. S., Bancroft, S., & Ahearn, W. H. (2008). A comparison of most-to-least and least-to-most prompting on the acquisition of solitary play skills. Behavior Analysis in Practice, *1*(1), 37–43. doi:10.1007/BF03391719

CHAPTER 9

Session 7: Bringing it all together

WHAT SHOULD I EXPECT?

Welcome to Session 7. This chapter outlines Session 7 for "Imagine, Create, Belong". Within this chapter, there are two main sections – Section A and Section B. Section A is for young people in their early to mid-adolescence who may be neuro-diverse and attend a mainstream school (Intelligence Quota (IQ) score is greater than or equal to 70). As this is possibly their penultimate session, this session includes a practice run-through of the group's negotiated movie. Section B is for young people who have additional needs and attend a special school (for those with an IQ score of less than or equal to 70). In Section B, Session 7 is expanded to cover two sessions across two weeks because young people with additional needs require more time to process the skills and concepts, for example, some activities are repeated from Session 6.

As in previous chapters, these sections do not need to be adhered to rigidly and you may choose from Section A or Section B, or a combination of both, depending on the needs, abilities, and interests of your group. You can follow the time suggestions for a 50-minute session or spread the session across more than one time period and take longer on the activities, depending on your group.

Session 7, this chapter, is organised in the following format. The aims of the session are outlined, then the underpinning theoretical approaches and abilities are listed with practical suggestions on how to approach the session (if applicable). Then Section A is presented. The facilitators' toolkit is provided, followed by a welcome to the group and the outline for the session. The activities are presented in the following format: a warm up activity; a tuning in activity; the action activity; and then the closure activity. Section A is followed by Section B. In this session, the warm up and tuning in activity are combined.

AIMS OF SESSION 7

- The aim is to bring the negotiated movie narrative together in a cohesive narrative with the group working together as a team.

- The main activity is overview and consolidation of plot, props, and scene, including music and sound effects, and practise acting it out.

- Continue to develop skills in working together, taking turns, listening to others, and staying on task. Flexible thinking continues to be challenged.

THEORIES, ABILITIES, AND APPROACHES UNDERPINNING SESSION 7

- Person-centred approach.

- Development of narrative that incorporates characters and props (narrative, theory of mind, representational thinking) (see Chapter 1).

Suggestions for approaching this session

This seventh session, Session 7, has a predictable, friendly atmosphere where participants have built trust with the facilitator to provide a safe environment where the young person feels warmly welcomed and accepted for who they are. The participants know the process and format of the group sessions. You can reflect the unconditional acceptance of your participants by commenting on what you see the participants do, for example, "You have been thinking about that for a long time. I wonder what the solution is". Continue to make a point of noticing participants' strengths and talents and drawing attention to these to ensure they feel valued for who they are and what they bring to the group. Neuro-diverse young people, while not a homogenous group, may have particular abilities and strengths not seen as often among neuro-typical groups the same age. Examples include, but are not limited to, thinking about topics in original and fresh ways; thinking deeply about topics; being able to focus on and remember details about topics they are interested in; being helpful, kind, honest, and generous; maintaining independent thought even when in a group. Work with the participants by contributing with them to refine the narrative of the movie.

SECTION A: FOR MAINSTREAM SCHOOL SETTINGS

FACILITATORS' TOOLKIT

Puppets

Pre-made characters from the modelling clay

Butchers' paper & pencils or felt-tip writing pens

Whiteboard

Movie director's clapperboard

INTRODUCTION

The facilitator welcomes the participants to the session and outlines what will be covered in this session. The facilitator reminds the group that this is the penultimate session. The facilitator may ask if anyone has any questions or queries from the last session.

WARM UP AND TUNING IN ACTIVITY (10 MINUTES)

Drawing me

This activity is the warm up and the tuning in activity. The group has now been together for seven sessions and, with a person-centred approach underpinning the culture of the group, the facilitators should have created an atmosphere of trust and security within the group. This activity requires trust of the participants in all group members and in the facilitators.

The facilitator gives everyone a piece of paper and a pencil. The facilitator asks the group to draw a picture that conveys who they are without writing any words or numbers. Let the group know that their picture will be shown to the group and the group will guess who drew the picture. Allow 5 minutes (or more if needed) for participants to complete this task. At the end of 5 minutes the pictures are collected. The facilitator shows the pictures to the group, one at a time, and the group tries to guess who drew it. Each "artist" (that is, participant) is invited to explain to the group how their work expresses who they are.

ACTION ACTIVITY (35 MINUTES)

Overview of the movie (20 minutes)

The aim of the action activity in this session is to finish the plot line development for the movie (that is, the narrative).

The facilitator goes over the movie plot with the group to ensure that all the points below are covered. The facilitator may use butchers' paper as a visual aid.

a. The story has a beginning (where the scene is set), a middle (where there is a problem to overcome) and an ending, which includes a resolution. Prompt the group to see if the group can extend the story further. For example, could there be another sub-plot in the movie? For adolescents who are neuro-diverse, be prepared, as a facilitator, for the possibility of new ideas to emerge. Adolescents who are neuro-diverse sometimes have issues with memory and so going over the movie plot with the group is an important part of this activity. However, they may also change the movie plot or add to the movie plot this session. As a facilitator, go with the ideas and creatively incorporate the ideas into the overall plot.

b. What are the problems to resolve in the story? How has the group decided to resolve these problems?

118   Session 7: Bringing it all together

c. Within the movie, what do the characters do and what do they say? What are the emotions of the characters? How do they express this?

d. What props and scenes are needed for the movie? Are the props ready? What other props need to be made?

e. Is there going to be music in the movie or sound effects?

Practise "acting out" the movie (15 minutes)

When the movie has been reviewed with the group, the facilitator then invites the participants to practise a run-through of the movie with the puppets and modelled clay characters, props, music, and/or sound effects. Each participant has one puppet and one modelled clay character that they have created. This session a clapperboard is used to indicate the commencement of the movie. Invite a participant to slap the clapperboard when everyone is ready.

In practising the movie, will there be a narrator? If so, who would that be? Is there a director? Who would that be? Who would be responsible for the props and scenes? Will there be music and sound effects? Who will take responsibility for these?

CLOSURE ACTIVITY (5 MINUTES)

The facilitator brings the group together after the practice and asks the group how they feel. Is there anything else that needs to be done for the movie? In the discussion, ensure that all participants are leaving on a positive note, with knowledge of what they have achieved and created so far.

Pack up and finish. Say your goodbyes.

SECTION B: ADOLESCENTS WITH ADDITIONAL NEEDS

Please note the content of Session 7 is delivered over two sessions for Section B. For convenience, the breakdown of Session 7 into two sessions will be referred to as: Session 7 Week 1 and Session 7 Week 2.

FACILITATORS' TOOLKIT

Visual schedule (see Appendix 3)

Participant storyboards, props, and characters

Camera (computer tablet with movie making app)

Objects, such as a pencil, key-ring, mobile phone, but also include some more unusual ones, such as a fossil, holiday photograph, or wig!

Dark coloured bag

INTRODUCTION

The facilitator welcomes the participants to the session and outlines what will be covered in this session. The facilitator may use a visual schedule (see Appendix 3).

WARM UP AND TUNING IN ACTIVITY

Object stories

Session 7 Week 1 and Week 2

This activity is repeated from Session 6 as participants will require multiple repetitions before understanding the task and gaining confidence or skill. The focus of this activity is to create logical narrative sequencing. Participants' confidence and skill for this task will increase each session; therefore, with each repetition, they will require less scaffolding and support from the facilitator to generate ideas and retell the story.

This activity is an extension of the object substitution activities because this time the objects need to be incorporated into a narrative. The facilitator has collected together several objects and placed them in a canvas or dark coloured bag.

The facilitator passes the bag around the group and invites each young person to dip their hand into the bag (without looking) and pull out one of the objects. The facilitator explains that the objects that have been chosen need to be included in a story. The first person to begin the activity uses the object in a story. If your group needs more assistance with narrative, then the facilitator begins the story with their object first. Then, the next person in the group takes up the story and adds to the story, incorporating the object they are holding. The facilitator reviews the story between each participant's addition to the story. This continues until everyone has contributed to the story. Encourage the group to move the story beyond their everyday experience.

ACTION ACTIVITY

Session 7 Week 1

In this action activity, the group continues to make props. The facilitator has collected the materials needed to make the props. The participants have begun to choose from the provided craft materials what they need to construct the props for the movie.

Facilitators and staff will be needed to support participants to generate self-initiated ideas for the props. This support is given using least-to-most fading, where the teacher "allows the learner a brief opportunity to respond independently on each training trial and then delivers the least intrusive prompt if needed" (Libby, Weiss, Bancroft, & Ahearn, 2008). Thus, after a least intrusive prompt is given, more support may be needed, so an increasingly directive approach in generating ideas for props using provided materials may be used.

For example, the facilitator could say: "I wonder what we could do to this box to turn it into a castle? Let's look at this picture of a castle, it appears to have a door and windows." Provide processing time with an expectant pause to demonstrate to the participant that they can provide a response.

Participants who have finished their props are supported by the facilitator and/or staff to rehearse their stories with the facilitator or peer.

Session 7 Week 2

By this session, the participants may be at different stages of readiness to rehearse their movie. The facilitator may create smaller groups within the larger group, based on what stage the participants are at in their movie development.

The facilitator begins filming participants who have created their props and can now rehearse their movie narrative. These participants have an understanding of the presented concepts and can re-enact their movie.

For the participants who have finished their props, the facilitator supports them to rehearse their stories with another staff member or peer. The participants are encouraged to introduce their story before acting it out, and to use their participant storyboards and props to support their description or retell of the movie story.

CLOSURE ACTIVITY

Session 7 Week 1 and Week 2

Commonalities game

For these sessions, the focus of questions is preferences, likes, and dislikes.

The facilitator invites participants to sit on chairs in a circle. Ensure there is one less chair than there are participants. The facilitator then asks for a volunteer to stand in the middle of the circle and introduce the game to the group, reminding everyone of the rules (see previous sessions). The participant begins the game by posing the first question from the card (see Appendix 4). Once all the people who responded positively to the card are standing (for example, those who like cake are standing), the volunteer participant (assisted by the facilitator if needed) draws awareness to the differences between participants' interests and preferences. The volunteer participant then directs "Change places, go!" Individuals standing must find another chair in the circle to sit on before the volunteer participant sits. Whoever is left without a chair becomes the new leader. They have a choice between using a visual prompt from the bag or thinking of their own criteria. The game continues until the session time is up or all prompts have been used.

Invite participants to provide feedback on their experiences, including their perceptions of the process. Facilitators to provide forced choice options to assist participants to reflect on challenges and positive aspects, for example, "What did you like best? Making your character or filming your movie?"

REFERENCE

Libby, M. E., Weiss, J. S., Bancroft, S., & Ahearn, W. H. (2008). A comparison of most-to-least and least-to-most prompting on the acquisition of solitary play skills. *Behavior Analysis in Practice*, *1*(1), 37–43. doi:10.1007/BF03391719

CHAPTER 10

Session 8: The grand finale

WHAT SHOULD I EXPECT?

Welcome to Session 8. This chapter outlines Session 8 for "Imagine, Create, Belong". Within this chapter, there are two main sections – Section A and Section B. Section A is for young people in their early to mid-adolescence who may be neuro-diverse and attend a mainstream school (Intelligence Quota (IQ) score is greater than or equal to 70). As this is the last session, this session includes the filming of the movie and a celebration. Section B is for young people who have additional needs and attend a special school (for those with an IQ score of less than or equal to 70). In Section B, Session 8 is expanded to cover two sessions across two weeks because young people with additional needs require more time to process the skills and concepts. So, Session 8 includes both the penultimate session and final session for Section B participants.

As in previous chapters, these sections do not need to be adhered to rigidly and you may choose from Section A or Section B, or a combination of both, depending on the needs, abilities, and interests of your group. You can follow the time suggestions for a 55-minute session or spread the session across more than one time period and take longer on the activities, depending on your group.

Session Eight (8), this chapter, is organised in the following format. The aims of the session are outlined, then the underpinning theoretical approaches and abilities are listed with practical suggestions on how to approach the session (if applicable). Then Section A is presented. The facilitators' toolkit is provided, followed by a welcome to the group and the outline for the session. The activities are presented in the following format: a warm up activity; a tuning in activity; the action activity; and then the closure activity. Section A is followed by Section B. In this session, the warm up and tuning in activity are combined.

AIM OF SESSION 8

- To film the movie and to celebrate, drawing on participants' strengths and interests.

THEORIES, ABILITIES, AND APPROACHES UNDERPINNING SESSION 8

- Client-centred approach.

- Neuro-responsive social scaffolding.

- A narrative that incorporates characters, problems, resolutions, and props (see Chapter 1).

Suggestions for approaching this session

This eighth session, Session 8, has a predictable, friendly atmosphere where participants have built trust with the facilitator to provide a safe environment where the young person feels warmly welcomed and accepted for who they are. The participants know the process and format of the group sessions. This session is the final session, so the participants are aware of the group finishing, and the filming of the movie is the ultimate aim of the group. In this session, be aware of participants who may be feeling sad and do not want the group to finish. For all participants, it is important to have a celebration and so the closure activity this session is vital as a celebration of what has been achieved. You can reflect the unconditional acceptance of your participants by commenting on what you see as the participants' achievements, for example, "You have been working on this for a long time. Now it has all come together and the movie is finished". Celebrate with the participants by enjoying the filming of the movie and restating their achievements over the sessions.

If you are working in a community-based service and the group has been specifically designed and run so the participants would not normally see each other during the week, then closing is even more of an important aspect of this week. Participants may now be more in tune with their emotions and may recognise that they are going to "miss" the facilitator and other participants if they are only together for the group. If this is the case, it would be worth planning for closure from the first or second week with either a verbal or visual representation of how many weeks left. Participants should then be ready for closing by the final session. If they are ready for closing, then they will be able to enjoy the celebration and be ready emotionally to finish.

Examples of celebrations may include:

- a dance-off
- a cake, cupcakes, party food to share (if food is allowed)
- balloons and decorations
- a party game
- a goodbye song
- a certificate ceremony or speech.

SECTION A: FOR MAINSTREAM SCHOOL SETTINGS

FACILITATORS' TOOLKIT

- Video camera
- Characters created by participants
- Storyboards
- Movie director's clapperboard
- Movie props
- A memento the facilitator prepared, for example, a certificate

INTRODUCTION

The facilitator welcomes the participants to this final session. The grand finale! In this session, the film is made of the movie. The facilitator may ask if anyone has any questions or queries from the last session.

WARM UP ACTIVITY AND TUNING IN ACTIVITY (5 MINUTES)

Desert island

The facilitator introduces the activity by saying, "You've been exiled to a deserted island for a year. In addition to the essentials, you may take one film, one book, and one luxury item, which you can carry, with you. What would you take and why?" The facilitator then opens a discussion with the participants about what they would choose and why.

ACTION ACTIVITY

Filming of the movie (45 minutes)

This session is the culmination of all the work the participants have put into the sessions. If the group has allocated jobs to particular participants, then the facilitator encourages them to get set up for the movie. That is, setting up the props, getting the characters ready and in position, and cuing music and sound effects. If there are allocated roles within the group, the participants get into position. For example, is there a director? A narrator? A prop person? A person organising the music and/or sound effects? In summary, the group has:

- set up the scene
- placed the characters in position
- music and sound effects ready, if appropriate.

The person with the clapperboard indicates "Action" for the movie to begin. The facilitator follows the participants as the person who is filming the movie. The participants act out the movie and the facilitator follows. It is important that the facilitator does not take over this session and is a team member in the film making along with the participants.

CLOSURE ACTIVITY (5 MINUTES)

A celebration! After the filming of the movie, the group may have something to eat and drink. The facilitator has prepared a memento for each participant. This may be a certificate or small miniature. The participants take their modelled clay characters home with them. The facilitator goes around the group and asks the participants for any comments about the movie or what they enjoyed about the sessions.

The facilitator organises with the group how to get a copy of the movie to them, for example, the movie will be posted on a USB, or the facilitator will put the movie on a link and send the group the link. If the group decides to access the movie via a link, then the facilitator negotiates with the group how long the link will be available for them to download. The link could be to an unlisted YouTube video, One Drive, Google Drive, or so on.

Pack up and finish. Say your goodbyes and congratulations!

SECTION B: ADOLESCENTS WITH ADDITIONAL NEEDS

Please note the content of Session 8 is delivered over two sessions for Section B. For convenience, the breakdown of Session 8 into two sessions will be referred to as: Session 8 Week 1 and Session 8 Week 2.

FACILITATORS' TOOLKIT

Visual schedule (see Appendix 3)

Bean-filled toy

Strength cards (see Appendix 2)

Board game (for example, Trouble, Guess Who, or Uno)

Camera (computer tablet with movie making app)

Projector or large screen

Popcorn

Certificates

INTRODUCTION

The facilitator welcomes the participants to these final sessions and outlines what will be covered in this session. The facilitator may use a visual schedule (see Appendix 3).

WARM UP AND TUNING IN ACTIVITY

Session 8 Week 1

Throwing bean-filled toy

The facilitator organises the whole group to sit in a circle (on the floor or on chairs). The facilitator models orienting his or her body towards a participant, gaining attention and greeting. This may be done verbally, gesturally, or through an augmented communication system. When participants have imitated how to orient their body, the facilitator throws the bean-filled toy to a group member, while saying their name. That group member then throws the bean-filled toy to another participant, saying their name, and so on. The facilitator reflects any prosocial behaviour observed, that is, "I noticed you facing John".

Session 8 Week 2

Strength card introductions

The facilitator organises the group into a circle, either sitting on the floor or around a table. The facilitator puts out the strength cards in the middle of the circle and invites participants to select a strength card (see Appendix 2) from the middle of the circle. Then each participant is given the opportunity to introduce themselves with their name and the strength they have chosen – for example, "I'm Sally and I'm strong". Each participant has a turn. Option: the facilitator may also suggest participants express their strength with their body through facial expression or body movement.

Note: If, as a facilitator, you filmed these activities in initial sessions, you may wish to film these activities for evaluation purposes.

ACTION ACTIVITY

Session 8 Week 1

Carrying on from Session 7, the facilitator and/or staff film the remaining participants' movies. The facilitator ensures that all participants have had their movie filmed by the end of this session.

Participants who have completed their movie select a board game to play with peers, with support from the facilitator and staff where required.

Note: Facilitators may need to edit footage of participant's movies. It may be necessary or helpful to include text descriptions or voiceovers in the movie.

Session 8 Week 2

In this session, all the participants view their own movies as well as those of other participants. The movie viewing is with popcorn!

Before the facilitator shows the movie of a participant, the participant stands in front of the group and introduces their movie by reading their storyboard. The movie is shown. After each movie, participants are encouraged to comment on something they liked about the movie.

CLOSURE ACTIVITY

Session 8 Week 1

Commonalities game

The facilitator invites participants to sit on chairs in a circle. Ensure there is one less chair than there are participants. The facilitator then asks for a volunteer to stand in the middle of the circle and introduce the game to the group, reminding everyone of the rules (see previous sessions). The participant begins the game by posing the first question from the card (see Appendix 4). Once all the people who responded positively to the card are standing (for example, those who like cake are standing), the volunteer participant (assisted by the facilitator if needed) draws awareness to the differences between participants' interests and preferences. The volunteer participant then directs "Change places, go!" Individuals standing must find another chair in the circle to sit on before the volunteer participant sits. Whoever is left without a chair becomes the new leader. They have a choice between using a visual prompt from the bag or thinking of their own criteria. The game continues until the session time is up or all prompts have been used. This game is optional for Session 8 Week 2.

Session 8 Week 2

The facilitator invites participants to reflect on their favourite aspects of the programme with visual supports (see Appendix 4).

The facilitator hands out certificates to all the participants.

The facilitator and group then say goodbye to each other because this is the last session.

CHAPTER 11

Epilogue

Congratulations! You have completed your eight sessions of "Imagine Create Belong". By now, your group will have completed a movie together, and you will have shared this with them in a manner of their choosing.

You might find that participants express interest in continuing working together, particularly if the group was run in a school setting. It is very beneficial for neuro-diverse young people to continue being creative together to carry on their sense of belonging in a group. Developing a club or creative society will further support their social development and social skills and help them channel their energies in productive ways. Being part of a group where they are able to imagine, create, and belong on an ongoing basis will assist to maintain and further develop skills developed through the programme, such as communication, cooperation, empathy, engagement and self-control, and flexible and sequential thinking. It will also lower the incidence of problematic behaviours, such as bullying, hyperactivity/inattention, externalising (for example, acting out), and internalising (for example, negative self-talk) (Goldingay et al., 2015).

If the group was run in a school, we suggest discussing with the school principal if a space could be set up for the group to continue to meet informally, with occasional support from school student welfare staff or other appropriate staff members. This could include a room that is available at recess and/or lunch, where materials for developing stories and movie artefacts (for example, modelling clay, butchers' paper, felt-tip writing pens) are available. If staff are able to support this on an ongoing basis, participants may regularly frequent this space and continue the benefits that were initiated by the programme.

In addition, some participants may have discovered a flair for an activity they took part in, including movie production, for example, acting, improvisation, storytelling, creative arts, or sound effects. In your role as facilitators, it would be useful to source activities that are available in the community where your participants live, so that they could potentially continue to develop their skills. Examples of community activities could be located in clubs or interest groups, such as child actor studios, art groups, music groups, or creative art courses run by local communities. By encouraging participants to continue their enjoyment of creating in a community group, you will further enable belonging of the young person within their community.

REFERENCE

Goldingay, S., Stagnitti, K., Sheppard, L., McGillivray, J., McLean, B., & Pepin, G. (2015). An intervention to improve social participation for adolescents with autism spectrum disorder: Pilot study. *Developmental Neurorehabilitation*, *18*(2), 122–130. doi:10.3109/17518423.2013.855275

APPENDIX 1

Blank storyboard sheets

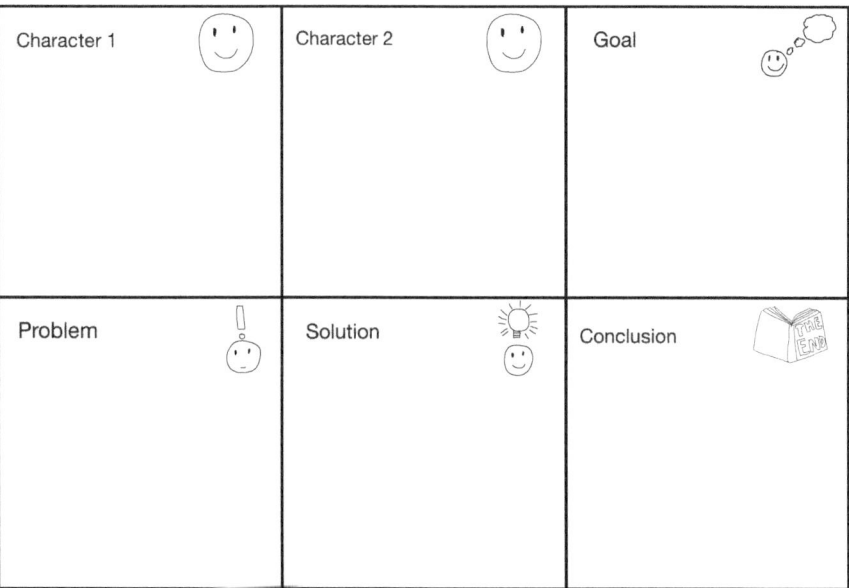

Figure A1.1 *Storyboard example*

APPENDIX 2

Strength cards

Strength cards are cards with the visual prompts and/or vocabulary. They are an aid for participants to begin exploring personal characteristics and defining who they are at their best. There are cards that are commercially available. Cards can also be made by facilitators.

Facilitator-created cards would be cards with a picture, graphic, and single word or simple phrase – whichever is suitable for the participants in the programme. Examples of cards include:

"I am strong"

"I am caring"

"I am creative"

"I am tall"

"I can dance"

APPENDIX 3

Visual schedule

Throughout the programme, it will be helpful to follow a visual schedule to support participants to understand and engage with the programme. Below is information relating to three different schedules to suit various participants' needs. Information has been adapted from Brady et al. (2016). Brady et al. (2016) note that participants have the right know what to expect from a programme and also have a right to be spoken to and not about (National Joint Committee for the Communication Needs of Persons with Severe Disabilities, 1992).

WHY SCHEDULES?

Visual schedules provide predictability or opportunity for participants to anticipate the sequence of events in the programme.

Many participants demonstrate symptoms of anxiety. When anxious, participants find it difficult to learn and remember information, attend to others, and behave within expectations.

Visual schedules are concrete reminders of what we are doing/what is coming up next/what is finished. Visual schedules can be used by facilitators to show: "This is finished. This is what we're doing. This is what's next."

WHY VISUAL?

Many participants may be strong visual learners (rather than strong auditory processors).

Providing a consistent visual cue for an activity in the programme will cue in participants to the expectations of the activity. For example, this is a tea party. During a tea party we sit at the table, I will get a biscuit and a drink. I have to wait my turn and use my communication system to ask for a biscuit, drink, and help.

Participants who experience the following may have difficulty with verbal direction or instruction.

- Poor language comprehension (understanding of words we use).

- Auditory processing (accurately hearing all relevant sounds delivered versus background noise).

- Poor listening skills (difficulty attending to the relevant auditory stimulus).

- Auditory memory (remembering what they have heard).

HOW TO USE A VISUAL SCHEDULE

To create a visual schedule, create a graphic, picture, or photo of the activities that will be in the session (for instruction on using a visual schedule, see https://youtu.be/ESMSiQ-mRE8). Place the graphics, pictures, or photos in the order in which they will be carried out in the session. Show the participants all the graphics, pictures, or photos of the activities to be carried out in the session. Begin with the first graphic, picture, or photo. When this activity is complete then:

1. Go to the visual schedule.

2. Remove the top picture (place in "finished" box).

3. Put the next picture in "current activity" location.

4. Carry out the activity.

5. At the end of the activity, return to the visual schedule: "We have finished X, now it is time for 2X."

6. Place "current activity" picture in "finished" box.

Visual schedule for the whole group

"This is what the group is doing today."

Show the participants the graphics, pictures, or photos of the activities for the session.

This should explain what will be happening and in what order.

Visual schedule for an individual within the group

"This is all the activities specific to you, you own this schedule, and you will follow it with support from us."

Depending on your participants, some participants will benefit from an individual schedule, which outlines their specific activities within the programme. For example, special activities that only they participate in, such as transition activities specific to that participant. This individual visual schedule allows the participant to exercise control over their day and can assist in transitions from one activity to the next.

REFERENCES

Brady, N., Bruce, S., Goldman, A., Erickson, K., Mineo, B., Obletree, D., ..., & Wilkinson, K. (2016). Communication services and supports for individuals with severe disabilities: Guidance for assessment and intervention. *American Journal on Intellectual and Developmental Disabilities*, *121*(2), 121–138.

National Joint Committee for the Communication Needs of Persons with Severe Disabilities (1992). Guidelines for meeting the communication needs of persons with severe disabilities. *American Speech and Hearing Association*, *34*(Supplement 7, March), 1–8.

APPENDIX 4

Visual supports

Use the graphics, pictures, or photos from your visual schedule (see Appendix 3) to provide a visual support during each closure activity. Invite participants to select their favourite activity from the visual schedule depending on their ability.

VISUAL PROMPT CARDS FOR THE COMMONALITIES ACTIVITY

The cards for the closure activity in Section B, commonalities, should be made to reflect the interests of your group. Provide up to 20 picture or text cards with a statement such as "I like dogs". Select a range of known preferred and non-preferred activities for your participants, to prompt discussion of likes and dislikes within the group.

Some examples include:

- I like my computer tablet
- I like Lego
- I like pizza
- I like broccoli
- I like cake
- I wear shoes
- I have black hair

You may also wish to complete Table A4.1 with images appropriate for your group. Images can be sourced from paid programmes or online, or could be photos you have taken. For facilitators who are speech pathologists, you may wish to provide aided language stimulation by pointing to relevant words while describing each box. For participants who use a personal Augmentative and Alternative Communication (AAC) system, it is advised that the facilitator familiarises themselves with the locations of the vocabulary in Table A4.1 on this system.

Table A4.1 Chat board example

I	Box	Big	Loud
My	Play	Medium	Quiet
You	Like	Small	Fast
Your	Not	Round	Slow
We		Square	

APPENDIX 5

Genogram, ecomap, and Tree of Life

GENOGRAM AND ECOMAP

Start with those in your life who you see as family, then consider other people and activities that are important to you – see the example in Figure A5.1.

TREE OF LIFE

See the example in Figure A5.2. Step 1: It is time now to go outside and have a look at the trees around you. Which tree are you attracted to? Does a tree show a connection to your journey? Grab a leaf, crush it, rub it in your hand, then smell the essence of the leaf. Make a note of the markings on the tree and the strengths of the tree. Take a photo of yourself hugging the tree and climbing the tree. Share with the group why you chose the tree.

Step 2: Now, draw your tree. The roots of your tree represent culture, traditional connection, identity, totem, and ancestry. Write these in. On the trunk of your tree, write in family: grandparents, aunties and uncles, siblings, cousins. Then, on the branches, put in your strengths, your community, your talents and skills, sports, achievements, education, kinship. On the leaves, write in important people, people who inspire you, and the strengths they bring to your life and your family or community. Include the fruits of your tree: your personal strengths, your hopes, your dreams, and your aspirations. Now, draw the sun. In the sun, write one word to describe yourself.

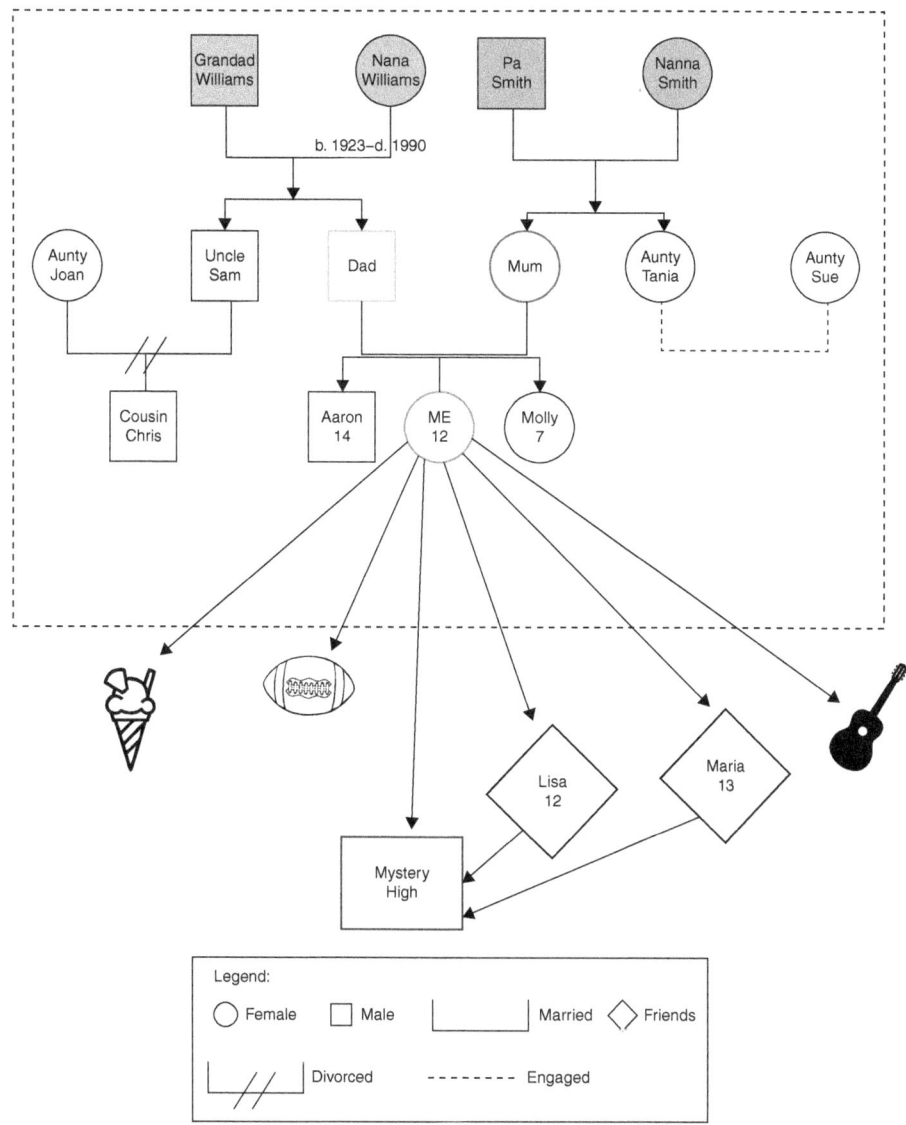

Figure A5.1 Genogram and ecomap

Figure A5.2 Tree of Life
Source: Created by and used with permission from Corrina Eccles, Wadawurrung Traditional Owner

APPENDIX 6

Character cards or choice cards

Complete Table A6.1 with images appropriate for your group. Images can be sourced from paid programmes, online, or from photos. Provide aided language stimulation by pointing to relevant words while describing characters. These prompts can be used when participants are describing their own physical characteristics to the group. For participants who use a personal Augmentative and Alternative Communication (AAC) system, it is advised that the facilitator familiarises themselves with the locations of the vocabulary in Table A6.1 on this system.

Table A6.1 Character cards or choice cards

Height	Short	Medium	Tall
Hair	Short	Medium	Long
	Straight	Curly	
	Brown	Black	Blonde
	Red	Something different	
Eyes	Blue	Green	Brown
	Wears glasses	No glasses	

APPENDIX 7

Goal and problem cards

Table A7.1 gives a list of example goals and problems for stories. These examples should be personalised for your group based on their interests or personal challenges, for example, listening to the teacher, etc. Write these on separate cards and use graphics or photos if preferred.

Table A7.1 Goal and problem cards

Goal	Problem
I want to play on my computer tablet	Tablet is broken
I want to go to basketball	The bus is broken down
I want to play on the bikes	The shed is locked
I want to buy a drink	I don't have enough money
I want a lunch order	I forgot my money
I want to keep playing	But it's time for bed
	But the bell has rung
	But I have to go to class
I want to play my computer game	My friend wants to play something different

Index

Note: Page numbers in **bold** refer to tables and in *italics* to figures.

AAC (Augmentative and Alternative Communication) 27, 30, 35, 48, 65, 139, 143
Abilities Based Learning & Education Support (ABLES) Speaking and Listening assessment 17
Aboriginal and Torres Strait Islander peoples: cultural safety 59, 64; identity 3–4, 9
activities, skills and 32–35
additional needs (underlying assumptions) 15
ADHD (Attention Deficit Hyperactivity Disorder) 1, 6, 25
adolescence: and neuro-diversity 6; in Western culture 3–5
Ahearn, W. H. 111
aims 26–28
alternative thinking game 74–75
Animated Movie Test 8
anxiety 5, 7, 135
ASD (Autism Spectrum Disorder) 1, 6, 7
Attention Deficit Hyperactivity Disorder *see* ADHD
auditory memory 136
auditory processing 136
Augmentative and Alternative Communication *see* AAC
Autism Spectrum Disorder *see* ASD
autobiographical memory 4, 9
Axline, V. 1, 12–13; basic principles 13

balloons 43–44
Bancroft, S. 111
beanbag greetings 63
bean-filled toy, throwing 47–48, 128
Bodkin, F. 9
Brady, N. et al. (2016) 135
brainstorming: character problem solving 111; context, plot and props 85, 86; narrative and identity 72–73, 75, 76; participants' and character's story 57, 62; problem identification 97–98, 101, 102; setting the scene 50–51
Brown, S. 8

CBT (Cognitive Behavioural Therapy) 6
CCN (Complex Communication Needs) 16, 26, 30
character cards (choice cards) 143
character development 27, 55, 59–60, 88
chat boards 49, **139**
choice cards *see* character cards
client-centred therapy (later person-centred therapy) 12
cognitive development 4–5; play theories 1
collectivism 3
commonalities game: character problem solving 112; conclusion of process 121–122, 129–130; context, plot and props 91–92; narrative and identity 78–79; participants' and character's story 65–66; problem identification

102–103; setting the scene 52–53; visual prompt cards for 138–139
community-based services 42, 125
Complex Communication Needs *see* CCN
congruence 12, 29
consequential thinking 17, 59
context 80, 87
counselling 59, 64
cultural safety 59, 64

Davidson, D. 15
depression 7
desert island activity 126
D'harawal people 9
Donovan, M. 9
drawing 116–117
Durie, M. 3

early play behaviour 16
Eccles, C. 9
ecomaps 41, 56, 59, 64, 86–87, *141*
embodiment (embodied cognition) 6
emotions, adolescence 4
empathic reflection 13, 29, 56
empathic understanding 12, 29
empathy 13, 27, 33, 59
Erikson, E. 3
executive function 6

facilitators 29–30
false beliefs 10, 58, 77–78
filming of movie 126–127
flexible thinking *see* object substitution
Francis, E. 15
Freud, A. 3

genograms 56, 59, 64, 68, 72–73, 86–87, 140–*141*
"geological layers" (Vygotsky) 11, 32–33
goal cards 144
goal writing 91
goals 50–51, 89–91, 101–102, 144
Goldingay, S. et al. (2015) 6, 8
Göncü, A. 8
Gray, P. 7

group bonding 55
Gumbaynggirr people 9

hypothetical-deductive reasoning 5

identity 3–4, 9, 140–*142*; narrative and 67–79
improvisation 87
individualism, Western 3
informal continuation 131–132
IQ (Intelligence Quota) 2, 16, 30

Knick Knack (video) 101
Koori people 4

language comprehension 136
Learn to Play Therapy 2, 15, 32
Libby, M. E. 111
Liddle, B. 97
linguistic competence 5–6, 35
listening skills 136

Maori people 3
Meador, B. D. 12
memory capacity: and approach 6, 43, 71, 60, 87, 97, 110, 117; increased 44
modelling clay characters 46, 59, 72, 86, 88, 98, 127; and practising the movie 118
movie: "acting out" 118; character development 27, 55, 59–60, 88; filming 124–127; introduction to 45–46, 49–51; narrative 33, 67–79, 94; overview 117–118; plot structure 81–82, 86–88, 98, 109–109, 117–118; props 12, 15, 104, 120, 111–112, 118, 120–121; scenes 87, 98, 118; script 109; theory of mind 57–58
multimodal communication 35

narrative: development of 33; and identity 67–79; negotiated 94
narrative ability 5–6, 8–9
Nettle, D. 97
Neuro-responsive social scaffolding 15
New Zealand 3
Nippold, M. A. et al. (2014) 5, 9

non-directive play therapy 12
non-judgementalism 12, 13

object stories 100, 107, 110–111, 119–120
object substitution (flexible thinking)
    9–10, 27, 34, 71–72, 107
oral language ability 5–6
O'Sullivan, L. 8
outcomes, long term 27

pace 13, 14, 15
Perone, A. 8
person-centred approach 1, 12–15, 33, 34,
    116–117
personal autonomy, in Western culture 3
play-based approach 7
plot structure 81–82, 86–88, 98, 109–109,
    117–118
positive regard 12, 29
Post-Traumatic Stress Disorder *see* PTSD
postcards 62–63, 89
Powell, M. B. 5
preference game 82–84
preparation 35–36
pretend play 1, 2, 6–11, 15, 26–27,
    28, 32–35
Pretending with objects (Stagnitti) 57
Priest. N. et al. (2012) 4
prisoners, young 1–2
problem cards 89, 144
problem writing 91
problem solving 11, 13, 16, 32,
    91, 107–108, 144; identification
    of 93–103
prompt cards, visual 53, 65, 78,
    138–139
props 12, 15, 104, 120, 111–112, 118,
    120–121
PTSD (Post-Traumatic Stress Disorder) 1
puppets 64–65, 77, 98, 100–101, 118

rapport 13, 14
reciprocal action 8
reciprocal dialogue 8
recursive thinking 10–11
reflective activity 99, 109

relationships, building of 33
repetition 15, 17
representational thinking 7, 10, 15, 26, 34,
    85, 97–98
risky behaviour 17
Rogers, C. 1, 12
role play 6, 72–73, 85–86, 98

safe spaces 43, 47
scenes 87, 98, 118
sensory processing 34
separation from family 3
sequential thinking 16–17, 25, 27
Shea, G. 9
Snow, P. C. 5
social belonging 3–5
social constructivism 1, 7, 11–12, 15, 34
social context 10, 11, 16, 27
social interaction: and development of
    narrative 33, 34; neuro-diversity and
    1–18; person-centred approach 12–14;
    social constructivism and 11–12; social
    scaffolding 34; theory of mind 32
social isolation 5
social scaffolding 14, 15, 34
special schools 2, 25, 27, 30, 35
Stagnitti, K. 8, 10, 57
storyboards 45, 50, 65, 87, 90–91,
    101–102, *133*
The Storyteller (game) 9
strength cards 48, 128–129, 134
support, least-to-most fading 111
symbolic materials games: narrative and
    identity 68, 70–72, 74–75; participant
    and character story 57, 62; representation
    thinking 85, 97–98
symbols in pretend play 9–10

theory of mind 10–11, 33; context,
    plot and props 84–85; false-belief
    scenario 77–78; and neuro-diversity 6, 7;
    participant and character story 57–58;
    pretend play and 8; problem solving and
    100–101; skills 32
theory of mind game 70–71, 96–97,
    100–101

Tree of Life 9, 56, 59, 64, 86–87, 140, *142*
trust 56, 68–69, 117

unconditional acceptance 13, 14; demonstration of 41, 56, 69, 82, 95, 105–106, 115, 124
unconditional positive regard 29

Valle, A. et al. (2015) 10–11
Vaughan, C. 8
visual choice boards 53
visual cues 136
visual schedules 135–137
visual supports 64, 138–139

Visually Supported Communication/Visually Mediated Communication 35
Vygotsky, L. 1, 11, 32, 33, 34

Wadawurrung people 9
Web Game 69–70, 75–76, 95–96
Weiss, J. S. 111
Whitebread, D. 8
woodblock characters 76

youth justice system 17

zone of proximal development 11, 15, 31, 33, 34